CREATED
for
INFLUENCE

"When Will began sharing with me the revelation God was giving him about influence, I knew immediately it would become a book. The material was far too rich and insightful not to be shared with a broader audience. You now have the privilege of partaking of this important and helpful information. The journey will be a pleasurable and fulfilling one!"

> **Dutch Sheets**, best selling author
> and international speaker;
> former executive director,
> Christ For The Nations Institute, Dallas

"*Created for Influence* is a watershed book that will mark you for life. Its principles will cause you to shift into a new paradigm in your thinking. If you put what Will teaches into practice, you will release success in every part of your life."

> **Cindy Jacobs**, president and co-founder,
> Generals International

"With brilliant insight, my friend Will Ford unveils the true nature of how supernatural influence is wielded and even thwarted, and how godly influence can shape personal and national destinies when we understand how to partner with God. This book is written with revelation that inspires me to penetrate this dark, dismal death planet with the light of life granted to every believer in Christ, our bright Morning Star. If the praying Church can, like Esther, influence the King of heaven, then heaven has no trouble influencing earthly kings. After hearing Will speak and after reading *Created for Influence*, I have a greater desire to be like a star in the heavens instead of a mere celebrity on earth (see Daniel 12:3)!"

> **Lou Engle**, The Call; Bound 4 Life;
> Justice House of Prayer (JHOP)

"My friend Will Ford rightly captures a most important yet widely neglected reality: godly influence. If we study the heroes of the Bible, we see that most received the gift of influence and used it to transform their world. I pray that all who are in or aspire to positions of influence will read Will's excellent book."

> **Francis Frangipane**, senior pastor, River of Life Ministries

"Several years ago the Lord swept me through the glass doors that separate secular thinkers from religiously defined preachers. Unprepared, I did the best I could to seize my moment to speak to our culture through secular newspapers, radio and television, instead of the pulpit alone.

"Today I realize that God had given me a unique gift of influence. If only I had read Will Ford's book before my big moment came, I could be further along in my journey of social impact on our culture. This book plumbs the depths of fresh scriptural concepts with biblical authority, while giving us modern examples of winners who have used their influence well.

"If you are expecting God to use you in a mighty way, this book is a must-read. For the sleeping Church, this book should come with a label: *May be hazardous to your complacency!*"

Harry R. Jackson Jr., senior pastor, Hope Christian Church; founder and chairman, High Impact Leadership Coalition

"In this book, my friend and mentor Will Ford will teach you that a great call cannot be fulfilled without a great consecration. My life is the fruit of this message. It is with great joy that I recommend this book to you!"

Rick Pino, Heart of David Worship and Missions Center, www.heartofdavid.org, Austin, Texas

"Few people have understanding of the spiritual dynamics that create influence in the earth like Will Ford. In *Created for Influence*, Will unfolds revelation that has come through years of rigorous study and prayer. This book has challenged me afresh to take my stand in intercession to see the heavenly realms shifted in order that the earth may experience the power of the Kingdom of God."

Billy Humphrey, director, International House of Prayer Atlanta

UPDATED AND EXPANDED EDITION

CREATED *for* INFLUENCE

Transforming Culture *from* Where You Are

WILLIAM L. FORD III

Chosen

a division of Baker Publishing Group
Minneapolis, Minnesota

© 2007, 2014 by William L. Ford III

Published by Chosen Books
11400 Hampshire Avenue South
Bloomington, Minnesota 55438
www.chosenbooks.com

Chosen Books is a division of
Baker Publishing Group, Grand Rapids, Michigan

Printed in the United States of America

All rights reserved. No part of this publication may be reproduced, stored in a retrieval system, or transmitted in any form or by any means—for example, electronic, photocopy, recording—without the prior written permission of the publisher. The only exception is brief quotations in printed reviews.

This updated and expanded edition published 2014

Library of Congress Cataloging-in-Publication Data
Ford, William L., III
    Created for influence : transforming culture from where you are / foreword by Dutch Sheets ; William L. Ford III. — Updated and Expanded Edition.
        pages cm
    Rev. ed. of: Created for influence : releasing God's will for your life and nation. c2007.
    Includes index.
    Summary: "Created for Influence calls readers to transform the culture through intercession and action, breaking the power of personal and national strongholds"— Provided by publisher.
    ISBN 978-0-8007-9588-7 (pbk. : alk. paper)
    1. Influence (Psychology)—Religious aspects—Christianity. 2. Christianity and culture—United States. 3. Christian life. I. Title.
BV4597.53.I52F67 2014
261.0973—dc23   2014012871

Unless otherwise indicated, Scripture taken from the HOLY BIBLE, NEW INTERNA-TIONAL VERSION®. Copyright © 1973, 1978, 1984 Biblica. Used by permission of Zondervan. All rights reserved.

Scripture quotations identified MESSAGE are from The Message by Eugene H. Peterson, copyright © 1993, 1994, 1995, 2000, 2001, 2002. Used by permission of NavPress Publishing Group. All rights reserved.

Scripture quotations identified NASB are from the New American Standard Bible®, copyright © 1960, 1962, 1963, 1968, 1971, 1972, 1973, 1975, 1977, 1995 by The Lockman Foundation. Used by permission.

Scripture quotations identified NKJV are from the New King James Version. Copyright © 1982 by Thomas Nelson, Inc. Used by permission. All rights reserved.

Scripture identified KJV is taken from the King James Version of the Bible.

Cover design by LOOK Design Studio

In keeping with biblical principles of creation stewardship, Baker Publishing Group advocates the responsible use of our natural resources. As a member of the Green Press Initiative, our company uses recycled paper when possible. The text paper of this book is composed in part of post-consumer waste.

14 15 16 17 18 19 20   7 6 5 4 3 2 1

In Memory of . . .

A nameless teenage girl and those like her who saw fit to pass on the history of God's faithfulness. May the legacy of devotion to Christ of the previous generation forever influence our personal and national destinies.

Special Thanks

Special thanks to my father, William Ford Jr., for his amazing faith and courage and for instilling in me at an early age a love for the Word of God; and to Helen Ford, my mother, for her prayers and patience and for believing in me. Truly your influence as parents in my life has been immeasurable.

Special thanks also to my mentors Dutch Sheets and Lou Engle, and other mentors and friends for your insight and passion in helping me thresh out this message.

Also, special thanks to Jane Campbell, Andy Sloan and Anthony and Melissa Medina for your editorial genius and invaluable feedback.

Contents

Foreword

GOD GRACES YOU to meet certain people about whom you realize immediately that there is something very special. Will Ford is such a person. To be able to call Will a spiritual son of mine is one of the greatest privileges of my life thus far. I have taught at conferences with Will, driven across the country with him, walked the halls of Congress alongside him, fought next to him on the spiritual battlefield of prayer, housed him in my home and been in his home. I can tell you firsthand, he is the real deal!

It came as no surprise to me, then, when God began to promote him. Will is in such high demand that now he can barely walk the delicate balance of maintaining his business while simultaneously fulfilling his ever-increasing speaking schedule. I can assure you that the breadth of his influence is just beginning.

One Webster's dictionary defines *influence* as "the power or capacity of causing an effect in indirect or intangible ways." The effects of Will's life are already great, but they are nothing compared to what God has in store for him.

When Will began sharing with me the revelation God was giving him about influence, I knew immediately it would become a book. The material was far too rich and insightful not to be shared with a broader audience. You now have the privilege of partaking in this important and helpful information. The journey will be a pleasurable and fulfilling one!

We are living in a day when unusual favor from God is about to be released to those who have been faithful in the small things. It is a Daniel 7:22 season, following the enemy's war with the saints, "until the Ancient of Days came and judgment was passed in favor of the saints of the Highest One, and the time arrived when the saints took possession of the kingdom" (NASB). The saints of the Highest One are about to experience this heaven-decreed favor. This will result in broad spheres of influence through which millions of people will be affected for God.

On December 17, 1944, as a blizzard was raging in the Ardennes, General George S. Patton Jr. called on the Third Army chaplain, Colonel James H. O'Neill, to write a prayer for good weather. "See if we can't get God to work on our side," said the general.

"Sir, it's going to take a pretty thick rug for that kind of praying," responded the chaplain.

"I don't care if it takes a flying carpet," answered Patton in his blunt, no-nonsense manner. "I want the praying done."

The prayer was written, printed and distributed to every soldier in the Third Army.

Colonel Paul D. Harkins, who annotated Patton's memoir *War as I Knew It* (Bantam, 1980), wrote that on December 23, the day after the prayer was offered, "The weather cleared and remained perfect for about six days. Long enough to allow the Allies to break the backbone of the German offensive and turn a temporary setback for the Allies into a crushing defeat for the enemy."

Patton later said, "That O'Neill sure did some potent praying. Get him up here. I want to pin a medal on him." Chaplain O'Neill, the "prayer warrior," was given the Bronze Star.

In this hour, God is offering us favor to turn temporary setbacks into crushing defeats of the enemy.

Much is being said currently about the "saints movement" or "marketplace/workplace ministry." These phrases refer to taking God out from the four walls we call the church and out from behind the pulpit where He is preached once or twice a week. It is time for us to stop only "going to" church and start "being" the Church—taking Jesus into the real world every day of every week. For those who will begin to do this, the favor of heaven and the ability to influence many are waiting.

Read this book and digest its truths. Then do them. The eyes of the Lord are roaming back and forth throughout the earth, looking for those whose hearts are completely His, so He can show Himself strong in their behalf (see 2 Chronicles 16:9).

Are you one of those He is looking for? I hope so!

Dutch Sheets, bestselling author and
international speaker; former executive director,
Christ For The Nations Institute, Dallas

1

In the Grip of Heaven

THE STENCH IS UNBELIEVABLE. You quickly cover your mouth and nose, but it is still hard not to stare. The slab that was once an inviting pink color is now a slimy gray, crawling with maggots and buzzing with flies. Part of you feels a responsibility to at least throw it in the nearby Dumpster, but mostly you just want to get away from it as quickly as possible. Yuck!

Maybe you have never encountered a piece of rotten meat left in the elements for days on end. But this disgusting spectacle exactly describes the spiritual state of a culture when the Church does not fulfill her role as the "salt of the earth" (Matthew 5:13). Abdicating our responsibility of preserving the customs, institutions and general moral conscience that prevent a society from decaying will leave the culture to rot all around us. At times the Church stares in sickened fascination at what is decaying, longing for the Rapture, as God—and even creation—longs for our Savior to be manifest on the earth through us. "The creation waits in eager expectation for the sons of God to be revealed" (Romans 8:19).

The Church, particularly in America, is far more affluent than it has ever been in history. Yet our influence in the culture at large is much less than what it has been in the past and a shadow of what it could be. The tide, however, is turning. Divine favor is opening doors for individual Christians and entire ministries everywhere. Nevertheless, if we do not properly understand influence, we will not utilize this favor in the right way. This book, as you might have guessed, is about moving the Church from favor in society to its rightful place of influence. As you read, you will embark upon a journey that will radically transform your prayer life and revolutionize your walk with God. You were created for influence!

God led me on this discovery in a most unusual way.

A Divine Message

Have you ever awakened from a dream that changed your entire outlook on life? As strange as it might seem, God actually used dreams throughout the Bible to sidestep the limited human mind and speak directly to the heart of His servants (see Job 33:14–18). Sure, most of us will have dozens of "pizza dreams" for every "God dream" we experience, but that should not stop us from being open to what the Lord may have for us in these special encounters.

I had one of these encounters myself in 2003. In the dream, my spiritual father Dutch Sheets said, "You know, Will, God is teaching me a lot through this study on Ahithophel [pronounced uh-*hith*-uh-fel]." When I awoke, I said to myself, *Ahitho-what? Ahitho-who?* I had never heard this name before. I shrugged off the experience as a "pizza dream" and went about my business.

Several months later, during a time of prayer, I opened my Bible to 2 Samuel 15 and stumbled upon the name Ahithophel! *It is actually in the Bible!* I thought. Stunned, I upgraded the event from months earlier to a "God dream." I knew that Father God was about to teach me something very important through this man's life and story. I never dreamed, however, that this revelation would

1. change how I pray for the nations and governmental authorities (see 1 Timothy 2:1–2);
2. deepen my understanding of spiritual warfare and its effect on society (see 2 Corinthians 10:3–5);
3. increase my desire and gratitude for an intimate relationship with Jesus Christ, our King;
4. change how I see workplace and societal involvement.

As you read this book, I believe the same thing will happen to you. There are many things we do not understand about the unseen forces at work in our lives and in the world. Though the Bible is silent about some that we were never meant to worry about, God clues us in to forces and principles in this political drama that we must understand if we are to pray effectively and regain the influence God intends for us to have in the world.

In response to God's prompting in my dream, I began to study 2 Samuel 15–19—a story of betrayal, as prideful Absalom attempts to usurp the throne of his father, King David, by winning the hearts of the Israelites and then defeating him militarily. Absalom, having already stolen the hearts of many away from David by working gradually but powerfully at the city gates (see 2 Samuel 15:1–6), sees the need for Ahithophel's counsel to thrust him to the next level: Israel's throne. Once a trusted member of David's inner circle (see 1 Chronicles 27:33), Ahithophel betrays David by becoming Absalom's advisor. Fortunate for me, Ahithophel's name was only mentioned in my dream; he and Absalom were probably David's worst nightmare! Before America endured her Watergate crisis, Israel had her "Absalom-Gate" scandal!

Ahithophel is a brilliant strategist and political spin doctor. As you will see, however, his strategies reveal the powerful sway of the kingdom of darkness. How does King David survive this assassination attempt against his character and, literally, against his life? What makes him one of Israel's most godly influential leaders? What does this story teach us about biblical influence? As you observe the seen and unseen forces colliding in this story, you will understand how prayer and godly influence, properly wielded, can shape your future and turn a nation.

The Clash of Two Kingdoms

We must first see the vital importance of the two invisible kingdoms: the Kingdom of light (God) and the kingdom of darkness (Satan). Our rational minds sometimes overlook the fact that the story of the Bible is about an unseen God we accept by faith, angels and demons that are not visible to the naked eye and the forces of two kingdoms that influence the visible world in which we live. The unseen realm of the spirit, though we cannot see it, not only is real and active but has the ability to influence our motives and behaviors. Much of what happens on earth is affected by it, though most people, including Christians, give little credence to it.

We know that physical forces can be seen or unseen. If someone pushes you into the mud, for example, it is easy for a spectator to understand what just happened. But if your foot catches on a small crack in the sidewalk and gravity takes over, observers may think you fell over for no apparent reason. Just as the laws of physics govern the physical world, the laws of influence govern the spiritual world of human events. You see, sometimes unseen forces push our decisions and actions over the edge. Such was the case with Ahithophel.

Though Ahithophel is not a hero in this story, God used his role to help me understand the importance of maintaining a pure heart so that the right influence operates through us. What do I mean? Though it is not explicitly stated, a bitter heart might be the reason Ahithophel betrays King David. Their friendship and political relationship could have been strained because of David's adulterous relationship with Bathsheba. As the familiar story goes, not only does David get Bathsheba pregnant, but to cover it up, he arranges for her husband's death in battle and then marries her. (What a mess!)

As you probably recall, this is later exposed by the prophet Nathan, with the result that David repents and is forgiven by God (see 2 Samuel 12:1–14). By the time Absalom plans his coup attempt, many years have passed, but sometimes you never know who gets touched by the ripple effects of your sin. Why do I say this? Well, it turns out that Ahithophel is Bathsheba's grandfather (see 2 Samuel 11:3; 23:34). What a drama. Who needs TV when you have the Bible?

Now that we know more about Ahithophel's background, let's observe a vital part of this crafty plan carried out by Absalom and his followers. Watch as a simple celebration is manipulated into a euphoric victory parade.

> Then Absalom sent secret messengers throughout the tribes of Israel to say, "As soon as you hear the sound of the trumpets, then say, 'Absalom is king in Hebron.'" Two hundred men from Jerusalem had accompanied Absalom. *They had been invited as guests and went quite innocently, knowing nothing about the matter.* While Absalom was offering sacrifices, he also sent for Ahithophel the Gilonite, David's counselor, to come from

Giloh, his hometown. And so the conspiracy gained strength, and Absalom's following kept on increasing.

2 Samuel 15:10–12 (emphasis added)

How clever! This most ingenious plan created the perception of a rising public demand for Absalom to take the throne. The two hundred people were important for Absalom's image. What if they were some of the most well-respected people in Israel? Imagine sly Absalom walking with your

- most respected politician
- adored actor
- beloved teacher
- favorite coach or athlete
- godly mentor, father or pastor

If the people you most respect are walking innocently with Absalom, in the midst of this adulation with blowing trumpets, you could be swept in also. These A-list guests, unknowingly, are lending their credibility to the scheme. This key strategy is important. Listen, Ahithophel and Absalom know that the sight of these esteemed men walking with them will influence David's supporters and power base to follow Absalom instead. Combined with Absalom's clandestine supporters, they are able to generate enough momentum to sweep up the "regular folks" who have no idea what is going on. Using the laws of influence, this strategy gives just the right thrust. It pushes the idea of Absalom's rule over the edge onto David's throne. As if a poll has been taken, it is reported to David that "the hearts of the men of Israel are with Absalom" (2 Samuel 15:13).

As Malcolm Gladwell, author of the bestseller *The Tipping Point*, might say, Absalom reaches the "tipping point" of epidemic popularity. Though the chants are about Hebron, everyone knows it is a mere pit stop on his way to take his father's palace.

The plan works, and the collective mind of Israel is poisoned concerning King David's ability to reign. Mind you, we are talking about David, one of the greatest leaders in Israel's history. Entangled in a mess, his credibility shot, David has to flee Israel to save his life (see 2 Samuel 15:14). To say that David's approval ratings are at an all-time low is an understatement.

What an incredibly diabolical scheme! Absalom knows Ahithophel is one of the most important people to make this plan work. Though his motives for betrayal are not clearly revealed in Scripture, Ahithophel's advice definitely conveys the influence of dark forces.

Ahithophel's advice was once considered "like that of one who inquires of God" (2 Samuel 16:23), but now his counsel reflects the kingdom of darkness. This is revealed in his sinful and utterly depraved advice, as he convinces Absalom to have sex with his father's concubines, supposedly to strengthen his coalition (see 2 Samuel 16:21–22). How sick! He then devises a clever plan to assassinate David in a manner that would actually increase Absalom's following (see 2 Samuel 17:1–4). At this point, if a movie were made of Ahithophel's life, the title would be not *The Oracle of God* but rather *The Devil's Advocate*. The demonic grip of unseen hands definitely pushes him over the edge.

I thought I understood influence, until God prompted me to dig more after reading this story.

The Power of Influence

I always thought of *influence* as a verb describing how the credibility, weight or importance of someone affected people, situations and decisions. I did not realize that *influence* is first defined in Webster's dictionary as a noun conveying something substantive and tangible. Also, did you know that *influence* and *influenza* are related words? Until doing this study, I was not aware of this. We will explore other aspects and definitions of these words in the following chapters.

> The power of influence is in its subtlety, because many times we are affected by it without our knowledge of what is happening.

But first of all, we need to know that *influence* conveys the ability to sway others' thinking and actions, as well as the interrelated cause and effect of people or events (seen or unseen) upon each other. The power of influence is in its subtlety, because many times we are affected by it without our knowledge of what is happening. As you can see, these dynamics are manifested in the strategy adopted by Absalom and Ahithophel; an epidemic, flulike mass persuasion turned Israel against David.

What does God's Word say about influence? Although the word *influence* itself rarely appears in the Bible, the concept of influence is certainly pervasive in Scripture. One of the Hebrew words that does appear in the Old Testament and is translated as "influence" is from the Hebrew root word *yad*, which means "hand." This makes sense, because people who are under the influence of something or someone are gripped or captivated. Sometimes they even succumb to foreign control. This translation also conveys how influence, like an unseen hand, not only grips but also fashions, shapes and exercises control by moving a person or turning a situation. (See Daniel 8:25, where the King James Version translates *yad* literally as "hand," while other versions translate the word as "influence," "power," "agency" or "means.")

This works not only negatively but also positively. The good news is that through prayer and godliness, we can influence the invisible realm and partner with God to shape history on earth. As citizens of the Kingdom of light, we have influence, too, and it is more powerful. Every Christian wants to experience the benefits of God's salvation and the fullness of His blessing, and becoming aware of how to avoid and defeat the enemy's influence will help. As we will see, King David had a great understanding of this realm of influence in prayer. David's heart was in God's grip, and His hand influenced David's destiny. That is what I want—don't you?

Let's see how God's hand turned this situation and made a way out of no way for David.

In the Grip of Heaven

David does not discount the significance of influence in the temporary, visible realm. Knowing its importance, he takes Ahithophel's gift and ability seriously and prays specifically for God to counteract his advice. "O LORD, turn Ahithophel's counsel into foolishness" (2 Samuel 15:31). Shortly after, David meets his trusted counselor Hushai, who rushes to David's side as the nation stands on the brink of civil war. David takes the opportunity not to receive comfort but to send Hushai out, in a sense, like a CIA covert operative. Hushai, David's secret agent, pretends to align himself with Absalom and is actually able to undermine the counsel of Ahithophel.

When Hushai appears before Absalom, he is miraculously granted favor with the usurper. Instead of suspecting him, the men of Israel accept his counsel instead of Ahithophel's. "Absalom and all the men of Israel said, 'The advice of Hushai the Arkite is better than that of Ahithophel'" (2 Samuel 17:14). David's enemies become his footstool on earth because the influence shifts in the unseen heavens. Powerful!

If Absalom follows Ahithophel's advice, he ultimately will triumph. Instead, David's outnumbered warriors are miraculously granted supernatural victory (we will discuss this more in the next chapter). David keeps his throne, and Absalom is killed in battle, after being found in a bizarre predicament. The Bible says that as Absalom rides his mule under the thick branches of an oak tree, his head gets caught in the tree, and his body becomes suspended, "hanging between heaven and earth" (2 Samuel 18:9 NASB).

From the way the passage reads, we are actually clued in to the unseen battle. Ironically, the evil head or dark source of Absalom's influence is just as bound in the invisible realm. Because David grips the heart of God in prayer, God, by His hand (*yad*), grips David's enemies—and what is bound in heaven is bound on earth (see Matthew 16:19). Prideful Absalom is "caught up" by his own web of deception, hype and Satan's influence. Ahithophel is so certain now that the rebellion will fail and he will be found guilty of treason that he hangs himself when he realizes Absalom and his men are going to follow Hushai's counsel rather than his (see 2 Samuel 17:23).

You see, when the Kingdom of God begins to manifest its dominion, everything begins to unravel in this situation. As a result, the devil can do nothing more for his pawns Absalom and Ahithophel. Being the betrayer he is, therefore, Satan does what he always does: He leaves them hanging!

There are a million reasons David's plan should not have worked. Why would Absalom disregard the advice of one of the most renowned counselors in the land in favor of someone else's advice? Why was everyone not skeptical of Hushai's motivations? The answer is that David understood influence from both kingdoms, and he knew how to pray. "The LORD had determined to frustrate the good advice of Ahithophel in order to bring disaster on Absalom" (2 Samuel 17:14). Wow! David's prayer released on the earth precisely what the Lord had intended to happen. King David shows us that if you understand the unseen influences at work in the earth, you can shut the door to their effect by appealing to the King of heaven and earth (see Isaiah 22:22).

We see that at the end of the day, it was not the opinions of men that mattered but rather God's opinion. You can have the best publicist or know the most brilliant strategist, but knowing God trumps it all. I am not against marketing strategies and the like when they are used in the right context and with the right motivation, but I do want you to know there is another "tipping point": when the prayer bowls in heaven reach their tipping point as God releases His influence in answer to our prayers (see Revelation 5:8; 8:3–5). Though Absalom and Ahithophel knew how to create fly-by-night trends and manipulate public opinion, it did not matter in the end. You see, Absalom and Ahithophel knew how to hype the masses, steal credibility and partner with men, but David knew how to partner with God.

Absalom's strategy worked so well that one of David's enemies felt emboldened enough to curse him openly and even threw rocks at him and showered him with dust (see 2 Samuel 16:5–13). But after God's man prevailed in prayer, this same antagonist apologized to David as he returned to Jerusalem (see 2 Samuel 19:16–23). The man basically represents the fair weather populace that hails you when you are up and nails you when you are down. You see, though public opinion had swayed against David, when the dust settled, the rocks were dropped and the cursing stopped because God made sure David remained king of Israel. David forgave the man, and the Lord, who sits in the heavens, probably laughed and wondered, "Why do the nations conspire and the peoples plot in vain?" (Psalm 2:1). God's will for David's destiny mattered more than the opinions of men, and it ultimately prevailed. David's destiny was influenced by the King of heaven and earth. From David, we learn that if you can grip the heart of God in prayer, God will grip your enemies.

Untangled from Satan's Influence

I want to take a moment to point out an important parallel here. King David, as a father, desired to share the kingdom with his son Absalom. He wept over Absalom's death, despite his betrayal, and said that he wished he could have died instead of his son (see 2 Samuel 18:33). This is exactly what God the Father provided for us. Seeing us tangled up in our sins and serving the kingdom of darkness, Christ did what King David could not do: He took our place. By sending His Son to die on the cross, God made it possible for us to be redeemed from the influence of the enemy's power. Jesus took our punishment of death, which gave us eternal life. By His resurrection power, He desires to grip your heart with His unconditional love. You see, the devil is a betrayer, but God will never leave you or forsake you (see Hebrews 13:5). Jesus is the Head of the Church, and of the increase (and influence) of His authority there shall be no end (see Isaiah 9:7).

Like David, have you ever had your reputation tarnished, been betrayed by others or gotten innocently entangled in a mess? If not, keep living—it will happen! I can attest, though, that if you faithfully stand with God in prayer, when the dust settles, you will be standing in your destiny. The principles I learned in this story helped me understand how to apply these concepts in my own life. They also helped me understand the dynamics of how God brought me out when I was entangled in a mess, much like David.

Many years ago, I was in a business situation where I was being forced to pay a great sum of money that I did not owe. A business relationship was destroyed when some twisted advice poisoned the minds of this company's executives concerning me. Influenced by their own "Ahithophels," this company was pressuring me with legal threats. Because of their influence, my reputation was tarnished with this company, and to make matters worse, they knew I did not owe the money but that I could not prove otherwise. These "advisors" had enormous favor and clout, and suddenly I did not. Legally, I was in a serious bind. I could not prove I did not owe the money due to poor record keeping, the details of which would take too long to explain. Suffice it to say, I was caught up in a web of deception. It was a situation where I had all the responsibility and no authority, or so it seemed.

Depressed and fighting back the suicidal thoughts and scenarios the enemy was throwing at me, I forced myself into a midweek revival service at a local church. Discouraged and depressed beyond description, I sat down, feeling all alone, fighting to last through praise and worship. But when the speaker came forward to speak, something unusual happened.

The evangelist walked to the pulpit, and before he spoke, he peered over the crowd of some fifteen hundred people and made eye contact with me in the middle of the audience. He then leaped forward from the platform and began walking briskly toward me without breaking eye contact. This was long before I did public ministry, and we did not know each other. I wondered, *Is he coming toward me?* About that time, a woman sitting in front of me stood up and threw up her hands, thinking he was coming to pray for her. He politely moved her out of the way, however, and said, "I'm sorry, but not you, ma'am. You, sir, step out in the aisle." He then laid hands on me and prayed.

I felt Christ's love coursing through me in a powerful way. With tears of joy streaming down my face, I asked the Lord why He had the evangelist single me out of the crowd. I will never forget His response. He said, *William, I will part a Red Sea to make a way for you, and I will part a crowd of people to let you know how much I love you.* That night my nightmare of depression, suicide and despair was broken. The moment I heard this, I knew that God was making a way out of no way for me. I have never felt that sense of hopelessness or struggled with suicide again.

With the newfound faith and assurance God had given me regarding this matter, I found that I did have authority over this situation—in prayer! I realized my battle was not against a large company but against the powers of darkness, and these people were pawns in a spiritual battle. Under the influence of God's loving assurance that He was with me, God began to show me key prayer strategies and how to partner with Him and take authority over this unjust circumstance. This was nothing that happened overnight; I had to stand in prayer for months while making myself vulnerable to intense scrutiny. But what did God do?

Eventually the company was scrutinized, investigated, audited and exposed for corruption. They later went out of business, and my so-called debt was canceled. God made a way out of no way for me. Did I pray for this company to shut down? No. But because God showed me key strategies for praying into this situation, what was bound in heaven eventually was bound on earth. The influence of the enemy was cut off, and when all the dust settled, I was still standing in the middle of God's will for my life.

Shaping Nations in Prayer

Is it not awesome to know that popularity and the fickle opinions of people do not matter? God is the author of your destiny, and He will give you, as He did David, the special insight into temporary circumstances to know how to pray. He will show you what is going on in the unseen realm if you are willing to draw near to Him as David did. This applies not only to individuals but also to nations. In the end, newspaper headlines only track temporary fads. The real question is whether or not the Church will draw close enough to God in prayer to rise to her rightful place of influence on the earth.

Just as with King David, God has a plan for our personal and national destinies that will prevail through us if we will stand the trial of faithful prayer. Isn't it a great encouragement to know that your heart and destiny are in God's grip? He will shape the destiny of loved ones, families, cities and even nations through your intimacy with Him in prayer.

As I have taught this message across the nation, people have asked me, "Is favor the same as influence?" The answer is that they are related, but they are not the same. Favor provides opportunities for us to use influence, but it does not guarantee we will steward or cultivate that influence the right way. Lots of people gain favor but have nothing to show for it in terms of lasting impact. They may shape trends or start fads, but they have no legacy when their fifteen minutes of fame are up. The purpose of this book is to teach you how to cultivate the influence you have and harness it to change nations for the glory of God.

> Favor may open doors, but influence changes nations.

Favor may open doors, but influence changes nations.

Let the Journey Begin!

We must remember that influence works two ways. At the same time God is calling you to influence nations, He is cautioning you to evaluate what is influencing you. As a Christian, you are called to change negative influences through prayer and action (see Romans 12:1–2). This book will equip you to do just that. You will see the influence you have in the unseen realm through prayer and gain a greater desire for God's love and intimacy. You will be equipped to recognize and remove negative influences in your life. Once you understand the principles in this book, like King David you will be able to triumph over the enemy's schemes against your destiny. You will also learn how to cultivate the character necessary to steward godly influence properly. Yes, character counts in intercession, and you will not have influence without it (see James 5:16–18).

We will also address the rotting culture around us by confronting the huge moral issues of our day. We will examine the effects of demonic influence and how to reverse them and transform the nation. As you read each chapter, I will share stories of how people just like you are applying these principles and making a lasting impact in their families, workplaces, cities and governments.

I believe this book is in your hands by design, and it is written especially for you. God is calling you to another realm of favor and influence to make an impact for the Kingdom of light through prayer and action. This book is not about how to win more friends or how to build a better network of associates. When we are under the influence of Jesus Christ and seek His Kingdom, however, everything else is added (see Matthew 6:33). Let the journey begin!

EXERCISING INFLUENCE *through Prayer*

Father, thank You for Your unfailing love and for untangling us from Satan's grip. Truly our destiny is influenced by Your hand in our lives. Lord, thwart the counsel of the evil one in my life. Break the enemy's deception in our nation, and turn us in the right direction.

As I read this book and reflect on Your Word, give me wisdom and revelation so that I can understand how to be a godly influence for You. Teach me how to pray. In Jesus' name, Amen.

2

Cosmic Traffic Cops

"A LONG TIME AGO in a galaxy far, far away. . . ." Almost everyone recognizes this opening line of one of the most successful film franchises ever. Of course, I grew up on the original *Star Wars*, before any of this Episodes I–III business, but that is beside the point. Fantasies like *Star Wars* play to our innate curiosity about the vast expanse we see above us every night. What *is* really up there? How far does it reach? Human beings have gazed at the stars for thousands of years and connected their incomprehensible brightness and distance to those unseen forces that we talked about in the last chapter.

Some in the ancient world believed that people are merely puppets in the hands of the stars that determine their fate. Others believed they could obtain favor from a star or celestial being and manipulate their circumstances here on earth. The Bible addresses these beliefs (for example, see Amos 5:26) and specifically forbids the practice of star worship, which lives on today in the occult and astrology. "When you look up to the sky and see the sun, the moon and the stars—all the heavenly array—do not be enticed into bowing down to them and worshiping" (Deuteronomy 4:19). As I studied, I was surprised to learn the word *influence* is connected to the stars.

As a matter of fact, one of Webster's definitions of the word *influence* is "an ethereal fluid held to flow from the stars and to affect the actions of humans." Isn't that intriguing? This definition is undoubtedly the basis of the King James Version's translation of Job 38:31, where God asks Job, "Canst thou bind the *sweet influences* of Pleiades, or loose the bands of Orion?" (emphasis added). You astronomers already know that Orion is a constellation and Pleiades is a star cluster in the constellation Taurus. Obviously, God is rhetorically asking Job if he can control the stars, and in doing so, He is reminding Job that He is sovereign over all.

Of course, today our technology has revealed that the stars we see at night are big flaming balls of various gases, which does not seem nearly as mysterious or romantic. Yet stars, because of their incredible distance from us, can symbolize something non-earthly, something that, like the stars themselves, is far above our current world. For this reason, God used stars—their light, their number and other fascinating qualities—to illustrate many important truths in the Bible regarding the heavenly or invisible realm. It is commonly understood, for example, that the one-third of the stars that are flung from the sky to the earth in Revelation 12:4 represent the one-third of the angels that fell with Satan. These heavenly beings, also referred to as demons, have a sweet or enticing influence—but an influence that in reality is corrupt. I believe that stars sometimes also represent God's ministering angels, which are more numerous than the fallen angels and which war on God's behalf, many times in response to our prayers.

In this chapter, we will look at biblical examples of these influences we cannot see and their resulting effect upon what we can observe in the visible world. Since God also uses the brightness and the vast number of stars to portray the influence of His people, you will also learn the shocking difference between being God's "star" and being a human celebrity—and which influences operate through the authority and gifting of both. The bottom line is that the Bible tells us there are indeed "Star Wars," but the question is, Who will win these wars in our generation: the kingdom of darkness or the Kingdom of light? Who will gain the prevailing influence and see it manifested on earth? Since influence conveys cause and effect, let's begin by putting on our spiritual glasses to discern the connection between the seen and unseen forces at work in our story of the conflict between Absalom and David.

God's Invisible Army

In the story of David and Absalom, David's military forces, though greatly outnumbered, miraculously defeated the massive army of Israel. This was an amazing supernatural victory and sequence of events. "The army of Israel was defeated by David's men, and the casualties that day were great—twenty thousand men. The battle spread out over the whole countryside, and the forest claimed more lives that day than the sword" (2 Samuel 18:7–8).

Wow! Talk about bizarre: Twenty thousand Israelite soldiers were scattered throughout the countryside, and the Bible says that more soldiers were killed by the forest than by the swords of David's men. Is that not strange? Allow me to arouse your curiosity a bit. Now, did trees attack these men, as in J. R. R. Tolkien's *Lord of the Rings*? Nope. (Tolkien, however, reportedly was so intrigued by 2 Samuel 18:7–8 that he invented walking trees that warred against men and put them in his trilogy.) Did these warriors run around in clumsy circles like the Keystone Kops and pummel their bodies into trees until dead? Humorous, but not hardly.

What could be the explanation? Could the ultimate answer be that God's invisible angelic army warred on David's behalf, similar to how this heavenly host marched before him in the tops of the balsam trees when God helped David defeat the Philistines (see 2 Samuel 5:22–25)? Though it is not clearly stated and we can only surmise, one thing is certain: King David had God's heavenly influence working on his behalf. As with other times in David's life, his prayer to God to thwart Ahithophel's counsel inaugurated war in the unseen realm. The unseen realm definitely influenced the outcome of this battle, and it will do so in your battles, too.

This concept is revealed more clearly in Daniel's intercession for Israel.

Daniel's Wrestling Match

During Daniel's 21-day fast, an angel visited him and said:

> "Do not be afraid, Daniel. Since the first day that you set your mind to gain understanding and to humble yourself before your God, your words were heard, and I have come in response to them. But the prince of the Persian kingdom resisted me twenty-one days. Then Michael, one of the chief princes, came to help me, because I was detained there with the king of Persia. Now I have come to explain to you what will happen to your people in the future, for the vision concerns a time yet to come."
>
> Daniel 10:12–14

As you can see, Daniel's fasting and praying on earth influenced the conflict in the unseen heavens. Why was there such resistance by the fallen principalities? I believe they were fighting to maintain their sustained influence over Israel, having convinced most to accept their captivity in Babylon as normal. This message to Daniel was important in shifting the mindset of the people and breaking the control of these dark powers. Before I go further, allow me to interject a point.

God makes it clear throughout the Bible that He is absolutely sovereign over the entire world, seen and unseen. He is King over heaven and earth. I am not trying to address huge theological questions such as why God allows evil. I just want to clarify the ground rules: God is not threatened, manipulated or surprised by Satan and his fallen angels or by fallen human beings. Nevertheless, as we see in Daniel's example, I cannot stress enough that the conflict between the two kingdoms is real.

Ephesians 6:12 reminds us that "we do not wrestle against flesh and blood, but against principalities, against powers, against the rulers of the darkness of this age, against spiritual hosts of wickedness in the heavenly places" (NKJV). Second Corinthians 10:3–5 gives even more insight:

> For though we live in the world, we do not wage war as the world does. The weapons we fight with are not the weapons of the world. On the contrary, they have divine power to demolish strongholds. We demolish arguments and every pretension that sets itself up against the knowledge of God, and we take captive every thought to make it obedient to Christ.

According to these Scriptures, unseen forces bend the will of human beings by infusing their minds with ideas and assumptions that are at enmity with God's truth. Applying this to Daniel's situation, I would observe that these dark "principalities and powers" naturally resisted God's message of hope. Through Babylon's education and government policies, these forces indoctrinated an elite Jewish workforce into Babylon's pagan ideologies and worship (see Daniel 1:3–5; 3:1–6). Though in the visible realm the Israelites labored for Babylon, ultimately they were acculturated into serving the invisible system of the demonic "prince of Persia" (see Daniel 10:20).

Daniel's 21-day fast, however, was a paradigm buster. It was another major crack in the stronghold of this "prince of Persia," which helped shift Israel's mindset from one of defeat to one of hope that Israel would once again become a nation. And as we see in the book of Ezra, because of God's faithfulness, that is exactly what happened.

Could much of the political and moral confusion, as well as the resistance to the Gospel, be due to fallen angelic principalities? Yes, their influence undoubtedly has impacted politics, education, religion and media, forming cultural strongholds today. As Christians, we must resist being acculturated into worldly beliefs, just as Israel did in Babylon, and remember that we are citizens of another Kingdom. Our prayers, like Daniel's, can partner with God in heavenly breakthroughs, resulting in openness on the earth to God's message of hope: the Good News of Christ's Kingdom (see Colossians 4:2–3).

Certain generations are pegged to shift prevailing demonic influences and strongholds, as we see in Deborah's intercession for Israel.

Deborah's Star Wars

Under the watch of the judge Deborah, an earthly battle occurred between Israel and Sisera, the evil captain of the Canaanite army. The Canaanites had dominated Israel for twenty years, and Sisera was as cruel and fearsome as any of them. In an act of incredible courage, a woman named Jael invited Sisera into her tent and drove a tent peg through his head while he slept (see Judges 4:21).

Cosmic Traffic Cops

This is another miraculous victory. How could a simple house-wife successfully assassinate the captain of an army as cruel as the Canaanites? In Judges 5:20, Deborah explains, "From the heavens the stars fought, from their courses they fought against Sisera." When I first read this, I thought, *Wait a minute! What do the heavens have to do with Deborah's victory? I thought Sisera was on earth. What do stars have to do with his defeat?* Remember, stars represent angels, good or evil, in the Bible. Deborah is telling us that her victory was won initially through prayer to God, as His angels warred against Sisera's demonic fallen angels, whose sick influence had oppressed Israel for twenty years.

You see, when the host of heaven was warring against Sisera from above, this mighty captain could fall by the hand of the smallest woman on earth. And the symbolic manner by which Sisera fell was important. Biblically, the head, or headship, represents rulership or authority that exerts influence (see 1 Corinthians 11:3). Therefore, Jael's driving the tent peg through Sisera's head is symbolic of the Canaanites' fearful rule and influence over Israel being broken. As a result, Israel enjoyed forty years of peace (see Judges 5:31) because Deborah knew how to exercise godly influence in the right realm first.

From Deborah and Jael, we learn that when you "stake" yourself to God's promises in your prayer tent, God will use your intercession like a peg to annihilate the enemy's influence. The seen and the unseen were affecting each other, and they still do today. Your intercession can break the demonic influence in your home, neighborhood, school and—with other intercessors—even a nation. As with Deborah and Jael, God's influence in your prayer life can stop the spread of the enemy's sick influence. Remember: *Influence* and *influenza* come from the same Latin root word.

Spiritual Epidemics

Long ago, rapidly spreading epidemics were believed to be the result of *influentia*, the influence of the stars. Plagues, for example, were thought to be the result of the stars' desire to make humankind sick en masse. Modern technology has revealed that germs and viruses are the culprits. More alarming than the bird flu, however, demonic "influenza" spreads from one infected mind to the next.

Now, there are many positive examples of how godly influence spreads through certain blockbuster movies and books. Often these release epidemic adoration of our Savior and advance God's Kingdom. Unfortunately, on the other hand, there are also demonic influences of media outbreaks, various book and film series and video games, that have spread a plague of anti-Christian and occult beliefs to millions of people. A billion-dollar pornography industry has also spread immoral sickness.

In other words, spiritual influence—good or bad—is contagious. Scripture reveals how demonic forces have deceived and will deceive entire masses by influence (see 1 Kings 22:19–23; Daniel 8:23–25; 2 Thessalonians 2:1–12). If you do not build up your resistance by renewing your mind, these thoughts can infect your way of thinking. You must choose to immunize yourself through activities such as Bible study, fellowship and prayer; otherwise, Satan's dark influence will spread an epidemic persuasion. That being said, we must realize we can partner with God and influence the unseen instead of being pawns of the enemy or puppets on a string.

Though much happens unintentionally, we must also learn to engage God intentionally for the release of His will and influence on earth. We do so many times without realizing it: through prayer, Scripture reading, praise, worship, fasting and other acts of obedience, as we saw in the lives of David the king, Deborah the judge and Daniel, one of the highest ranking officials in first the Babylonian empire and then the Persian empire. I mention their titles because God operated through their authority to release His influence in the unseen and seen realms. In this we see God's desire to operate through the authority He has granted us, using us as a godly influence in the world—whether on our jobs as managers or laborers or in our homes as mothers or fathers.

The angel spoke to Daniel concerning the end times: "Those who have insight will shine brightly like the brightness of the expanse of heaven, and those who lead the many to righteousness, like the stars forever and ever" (Daniel 12:3 NASB). As a Christian, you are called to be like a star that shines brightly in the darkness, emanating the very light and influence of Jesus Christ (see Philippians 2:14–16)!

God also used the brightness and seemingly endless number of stars to illustrate what He wants His people to be.

Man's Celebrity or God's Star?

God said to Abraham, "'Look up at the heavens and count the stars—if indeed you can count them.' Then he said to him, '*So shall your offspring be*'" (Genesis 15:5, emphasis added). God was not only talking to Abraham about the *quantity* of his descendants but also describing the essence of their *quality*. As heavenly citizens representing the Kingdom of light, God's people should be numerous and shine with righteousness. God wants us to be His "stars" and lead many to His Kingdom, like the star that led the wise men to Christ (see Matthew 2:9–10). In this way, we are cosmic traffic cops, directing people to the bright Morning Star, Jesus Christ. This is important, because people will be led one way or another. And, therefore, we must pray for leaders to be under the right influence.

Influence speaks not only of cause and effect but also of the release of moral or spiritual force, as seen in Joshua's battle with the Amalekites in Exodus 17:

> So Moses said to Joshua, "Choose men for us and go out, fight against Amalek. Tomorrow I will station myself on the top of the hill with the staff of God in my hand." Joshua did as Moses told him, and fought against Amalek; and Moses, Aaron, and Hur went up to the top of the hill. So it came about when Moses held his hand up, that Israel prevailed, and when he let his hand down, Amalek prevailed. But Moses' hands were heavy. Then they took a stone and put it under him, and he sat on it; and Aaron and Hur supported his hands, one on one side and one on the other. Thus his hands were steady until the sun set. So Joshua overwhelmed Amalek and his people with the edge of the sword.
>
> Exodus 17:9–13 NASB

It is clear to see that as Moses raised his staff of authority in prayer on the mountain, God's invisible force and power was activated as Joshua and the army fought below. Though this story explains warfare in the seen and unseen realms and their interrelatedness through intercession, another important principle is also at work regarding authority and influence. Through the authority God gave Moses, spiritual force was released, affecting everyone under Moses' sphere of influence. And Aaron and Hur played a critical role by holding up Moses' hands so that the Israelites prevailed. Powerful! Just as others upheld and supported Moses' authority, today we must pray for those in authority so that the right influence affects those within their spheres of influence.

Society needs its leadership to function properly, so, therefore, we are commanded to pray for all authority figures (see 1 Timothy 2:2). By the very nature of their jobs, such leaders have influence. As we saw with Ahithophel, influence in the hands of the wrong authority figure can bring much destruction. Why? Most people can be easily persuaded by a seemingly inborn fascination with the famous or powerful. Unfortunately, this fascination allows people who are not godly leaders to influence others simply based on their access to media exposure and fame.

All human beings are spiritual beings, whether they choose to acknowledge that fact or not. All of us are made in the image and likeness of God (see Genesis 1:26), and our spirits long to connect with the unseen world. Obviously, the right way to do this is to have a relationship with the true and living God. In the absence of this relationship, however, many people are unknowingly drawing on power from the kingdom of darkness.

The opposing reality is that plenty of people appear to shine, but not with the favor and righteousness of God. They are not stars, in the biblical understanding of the term, because they are leading people away from God instead of toward Him. Unfortunately, rather than true stars, they are mere celebrities whose favor and influence is from the kingdom of darkness. Whether they are self-indulgent actors, musicians or athletes, countless celebrities radiate an unseen influence. Do not be deceived; these idols do not use their influence to glorify and serve the true and living God, no matter whom you may hear them thank at the Oscars or Grammy Awards! While most of them rather naturally use their influence to increase their personal wealth and fame, in the worst cases, some intentionally deceive and sway those who look up to them toward the ways of the kingdom of darkness (see 2 Corinthians 11:14–15).

I want to be clear: I am not saying that every secular celebrity is demon-possessed or, for that matter, that every "Christian" leader is empowered by the Holy Spirit. It is not that simple. Nevertheless, a great number of influential people are knowingly or unknowingly empowered by the darker kingdom. They have accepted the offer of power from Satan that Jesus refused in Matthew 4:8–10. Remember, one definition of *influence* describes it as an occult power. Many people, from ordinary folk to entertainers and politicians, are willing to pay astrologers, mediums and spiritualists for influence. Of course, a lot of those occult practitioners are mere charlatans. Some of them, however, do have favorable access to fallen angelic "stars" or evil principalities in the kingdom of darkness, and aspiring celebrities seek their influence for prestige, power and epidemic popularity.

Clearly, a person does not have to be overtly involved in the occult to influence society with a perverse value system that expands the kingdom of darkness. We live in an age where people are so selfishly ambitious they will humiliate themselves on national television just for a shot at becoming a D-list celebrity! As the "god of this age" and "prince and power of the air," Satan is the current controller of this world's system (see 2 Corinthians 4:4; Ephesians 2:2; 1 John 5:19). As you can imagine, Satan is happy to reward individuals who are willing to pervert their God-given authority and gifting to advance his agenda, whether they know it or not.

As one small example out of the thousands I could choose, rapper Snoop Dog has certainly left his mark on pop culture. His music has sold amazingly well, and "for sheezy" (that is a "Snoop-ism" meaning "for sure") he has even influenced our slang! And what do we learn from watching this highly influential figure? Let's consider one of his hit videos from 2004, in which he

- shows a bag of marijuana
- verbally insults and degrades women
- expresses pride in being a gangbanger
- promises to murder anyone who crosses him

I have heard all the excuses for this malevolence, including the idea that rappers like Snoop are just "keepin' it real." Real or not, they have proven you can make millions exploiting other people's tragedies and extend your influence at the expense of others' misery. More appalling, Snoop was a paid spokesperson for T-Mobile, appeared in Chrysler commercials with Lee Iacocca and represented other major corporations. Isn't the favor he had strange? Why did Fortune 500 companies feel they needed the endorsement of a gangster rapper? Ask the king of darkness, whose influence—like the flu—is threatening to make an entire generation sick.

God is waiting for His children to "shine like stars" in the midst of this "crooked and depraved generation" (Philippians 2:15) and turn that generation in the right direction.

Let's take a moment to summarize the differences between man's celebrities and God's stars:

- Celebrities rely on earthly appeal or the kingdom of darkness. Stars submit to God and the Kingdom of light.
- Celebrities use their influence to benefit themselves; even their charitable works are self-serving, because they receive the glory. Stars use their influence solely to please God and benefit others; they are happy to serve in secret, and they give all the glory to God.
- Celebrities entertain people by saying what they want to hear. Stars provoke people by proclaiming what God says they need.
- Celebrities are swayed by public preferences and compromise. Stars are rooted in principles and unwavering conviction.
- Celebrities surround themselves with yes-men and entourages. Stars surround themselves with honest counselors and truthful mentors; stars are teachable.
- Celebrities hire public relations firms to hype and protect their reputations. Stars have died to self and, therefore,

to their reputations; they know that any light they have is God's light shining through them.

- Celebrities seek worldly success. Stars pursue godly significance.

- Celebrities use people to serve their authority. Stars use their authority to serve people.

- Celebrities use their influence to impress society's somebodies. Stars use their influence to empower society's so-called nobodies.

- Celebrities seek crowds and crowns. Stars seek God and lay down their crowns; when God exalts them, it is because of their humility.

- Celebrities build their own kingdoms. Stars build God's Kingdom.

Remember, celebrities may influence a fashion trend or a catchphrase, but stars are building an unseen legacy in eternity that can influence generations to come on earth. Either you can be a bound celebrity, enslaved to people's opinions and the kingdom of darkness, or you can be a star and rule and reign with Christ in heavenly places (see Ephesians 2:6).

> Celebrities build their own kingdoms. Stars build God's Kingdom.

What happens, however, when one of God's stars falls? He or she becomes a "church celebrity."

Church Celebrities in the Wrong Kingdom

Like our Lord Jesus, we all are tempted by Satan to accept ungodly power. Unfortunately, unlike Him, many Christians fail this important test. Jesus used leaven (or yeast) to illustrate how the influence of the Pharisees and Sadducees, the religious hypocrites of His day, functioned (see Matthew 16:6). Their focus on outward behaviors instead of internal reality created religious performers. They accomplished this through legalism and control—which turns people into actors more concerned with appearances—instead of grace and voluntary submission to God. Image is everything for church celebrities. When the way things look is what matters, the way things truly are will not be addressed, and the leaven of secret sins, such as the influence of sexual immorality, will begin to corrupt people (see 1 Corinthians 5:1–8).

Listen to what the Bible tells us about Christians who accept influence from the kingdom of darkness:

- They are full of compromise and sin (see Matthew 23:23–25).
- They teach false doctrines (see 1 Timothy 4:1–2).
- They are lukewarm (see Revelation 3:16) and carnal (see Jude 18).
- They are prideful, lack integrity and love money (see 2 Timothy 3:2).
- They name-drop to build credibility (see Matthew 23:5–7).
- They are crowd pleasers who are content to say what "itching ears" want to hear (see 2 Timothy 4:3).
- They bind people to man-made traditions (see Mark 7:8; Colossians 2:8).
- They are selfishly ambitious (see James 3:16).

Perhaps most frightening is the fact that, like the Pharisees and Sadducees, most church celebrities do not know they are being empowered from below. They do not check their own motivations closely enough to realize they are more focused on building their own kingdom than the Kingdom of God.

There is nothing inherently wrong, of course, with being well-known, whether you are a Christian or not. Nor do I have a problem with mega-churches and mega-ministries, as long as they do not water down their message to make it more comfortable for sinful people, rather than for the glory of a holy mega-God. Christians can become famous and stay faithful to God as long as they follow the principles of being God's star instead of man's celebrity.

Jesus was well-known, but He never operated like a celebrity. He truly is our bright Morning Star (see Revelation 22:16), yet He humbly "made himself of no reputation" (Philippians 2:7 KJV). Because Christ humbled Himself, His Father lifted Him up, and all people were drawn to Him (see Luke 14:11; John 12:32). He did not seek the crowds, yet the crowds sought Him. What Jesus sought was to please His Father who sent Him (see John 5:30). In His earthly tenure, Jesus possessed fame (see Matthew 9:29–31), but fame did not possess Him (see Matthew 4:8–10). There is only one "superstar" in heaven and earth—Jesus Christ!

James says that where there is envy and selfish ambition, there is also "every evil practice" (James 3:16). We must deal with our own hearts before we can even think of exercising influence over someone else. We must ask God to rid us of any vainglory, selfish ambition, pride, hypocrisy and desire to please people rather than God. We must also remember that our battle is not against people; it is against the darker powers that are influencing them. Yes, Jesus confronted people (particularly the Pharisees and Sadducees), and so must we. But remember, Jesus also wept over those same people (see Luke 19:41). Whether they are in the Church or not, our battle is to free others by praying and speaking the truth in love.

Esther: God's Star in Persia

The story of Esther illustrates perfectly how to be God's star in a situation that seems impossible.

The evil Haman had all the qualities of a leader influenced by the kingdom of darkness. "Haman recounted to them the glory of his riches, and the number of his sons, and every instance where the king had magnified him and how he had promoted him above the princes and servants of the king" (Esther 5:11 NASB). Haman was so prideful that he even forced people to bow down to him. When Mordecai refused to do so, Haman was ready to kill all of Mordecai's people—the Jews. Haman persuaded the king to call for the annihilation of the Jewish people (see Esther 3:5–11), and later he built a gallows to hang Mordecai (see Esther 5:14).

In response, Esther called the Jews to a three-day fast (see Esther 4:15–16). In the natural realm, she sought favor with her husband, the king of Persia, to reverse the decree. In the unseen realm, she knew she needed influence from the King of kings Himself. Because she chose to fight her battle in prayer and fasting ("Star Wars"), not only were the Jewish people saved, but Haman was killed on the very gallows on which he intended to kill Mordecai (see Esther 7:9–10).

Haman was a celebrity who loved fame and glory. He obtained favor with the kingdom of darkness, and from that realm, he was given authority to wield influence. Haman used his influence to intimidate and coerce people to respect him. He even knew how to use that influence to manipulate the decisions of the king of the mighty Persian empire. But in the end, it did not matter. Haman knew how to move the hearts of men, but Esther knew how to grip the heart of God. As a final twist, note that this young Jewish woman (whose Jewish name was Hadassah) had been given the Persian name Esther, which means "star."

Esther could have used her favor to save only herself. Instead, she put her favor on the line, fought in intercession and saved her entire nation. This same influence can operate through us today

CREATED FOR INFLUENCE

in the Church. The bottom line is that prayers that transcend you as an individual can grip the heart of God for your generation.

San Antonio: A Modern Esther Moment

On December 8–9, 2003, I participated in a strategic prayer gathering as part of the "50-State Tour" with Dutch Sheets and Chuck Pierce. As God would have it, this prayer meeting was in the "Lone Star State." Fifteen hundred people from all over Texas came to this important prayer occasion being held in San Antonio. Christians of many races, including Messianic Jews, Native Americans, Hispanics, African Americans, Asians and Caucasians, were there to pray. We began by repenting individually and corporately of our sins of racism. While this was happening, the leaders, including myself, sensed a shift in the atmosphere of the room.

During prayer, Chuck Pierce suddenly proclaimed, "Texas, the Lord would say to you that there is a nation in your loins." Shortly after this, a pastor came forward and said, "I believe the Lord has shown me what nation that is, and that nation is Iraq. We need to pray for the Fourth Infantry out of Fort Hood, Texas." He went on to explain how important the Fourth Infantry Division was, because it was one of several divisions tracking Saddam Hussein—who up to that time had not been found—during the war in Iraq.

Chuck prophesied these words: "'In this state tonight you will be able to decree to Babylon and that strongman who has not been found that he will now be found,' saith the Lord." Chuck and Dutch began to lead us in decrees for the exposure and finding of Saddam and to pray against all dark powers that were keeping him hidden. As these decrees went forth, tears were shed, and shouts and loud cries could be heard from those present. As someone who was there, I can assure you this was definitely

52

not something conjured up by human thinking but a sovereign invitation to partner with God and decree His will on earth.

Our prayer time ended with an African American uniformed officer coming forward and praying, "As a witness to the prophetic word in this house, as a representative of the armed forces in the state of Texas, I declare in the name of the Lord: It shall be." All of these things were done with great humility, boldness and the spontaneous leading of the Holy Spirit. We knew our prayers would be answered, but honestly, I was a little surprised at how bold we had become. We were declaring things that were measurable: They would either happen or they would not.

At the end of that week, on December 13, I received a phone call from a close friend. Without knowing about our prayer gathering, he said, "Will, you've been talking to me about the book of Esther, and I thought I'd read it today. When I picked up my Bible, it opened to Esther 9:1, which says, 'In the twelfth month, that is, the month of Adar, on the thirteenth day, the time came for the king's command and his decree to be executed. On the day that the enemies of the Jews had hoped to overpower them, the opposite occurred, in that the Jews themselves overpowered those who hated them' [NKJV].

"The passage goes on to say that it was the same day that Haman's sons were found and brought to justice," he continued. "Today is the twelfth month and the thirteenth day. We need to pray—something is going on!"

I did not really connect our conversation with our previous prayer time in San Antonio, but this friend has a track record for discerning the times, and I knew something significant was happening.

Everything made sense the following morning. Early that Sunday morning, I turned on my television and learned that Saddam Hussein had been captured alive! As the story unfolded, I was amazed to learn that the Fourth Infantry Division from

Fort Hood, which we had prayed for, was the division that had found Hussein and that he had been caught the previous day— Saturday, the thirteenth day of the twelfth month. As providence would have it, modern-day Iraq is part of the ancient Babylonian and Persian empires, where Esther lived. Both Haman and Saddam were known for their ruthlessness and brutality, and it could be said that a new son of Haman, Saddam Hussein, was found and brought to justice on the twelfth month and the thirteenth day—just like Haman's sons of old.

I am not sharing this to take credit for anything: We were just following the leading of the Lord. I want you to understand that God is inviting us to partner with Him, to fight on His side in the "Star Wars" and see the results here on earth. Influence in the celebrity realm shapes trends, but influence in the heavens shapes nations. I do think it is significant that there was repentance for racism in that prayer meeting. When God sees us unified, He commands His blessing to be released (see Psalm 133). The beauty is that when He sees us as one, He sees His Bride, and like Esther, we have the ear of the King.

We have a set of questions before us, however, as the corporate Bride of Christ: Do we want hypocrisy or holiness? Will we wink at sin in the Church or confront it? Do we want religion or the Kingdom of God? Do we want to be the world's celebrities or God's stars?

Amazing events are unfolding in our world every day. God is inviting every one of His children to move beyond the selfish desire for fame, power and worldly affirmation and to learn to pray prayers that will change the course of the future. In the next chapter, we will explore the pathway to this realm of influence: the love of God.

EXERCISING INFLUENCE *through Prayer*

Father, I humbly ask Your forgiveness for times I have operated as a celebrity. I repent of all hypocrisy, pride and selfish ambition. Your promise is that if I confess my sins, You will cleanse me; I gratefully receive the cleansing power of Jesus' blood.

Lord, I thank You that when I stake myself to Your promises in prayer, You destroy the enemy's influence. O God, as You did in Daniel's and Esther's days, raise up a fasting army that will pray until demonic strongholds are broken in education, politics, the arts and the media. Give us godly leaders in these spheres of influence. Transform Hollywood into "Holy-wood" by converting celebrities into stars in Your Kingdom. Shape our culture by Your influence!

Empower Your Church to shine brightly and lead many to righteousness through Your message of love and hope. Lord, break through any seen and unseen resistances by granting help from heaven. Jesus, our bright Morning Star, thank You for warring over the destiny of every nation. In Your precious name, Amen.

3

Under the Influence

THERE ARE CERTAIN MOVIE LINES that are so memorable that they become part of pop culture. Humphrey Bogart's "Here's lookin' at you, kid," in *Casablanca* is one example from a generation back. In a later day, Tom Cruise and Renée Zellweger acted out one of the most remembered scenes in movie history in *Jerry Maguire*. I am not endorsing this movie or the actors' personal lifestyles; rather, I want to reveal the underlying power of one scene and its famous catchphrase.

In this scene, Cruise's character, Jerry Maguire, is looking for his wife and walks nervously into a room full of women who are angry at him. In the midst of this hostile environment, he finds her across the room. He peers at his wife so intently that you can almost feel his butterflies in your stomach. Mrs. Maguire stares back at him, and it appears her speech is taken away because her heart is beating faster. In an effort to win her back, Jerry delivers a powerful, articulate speech expressing his love for her. Mrs. Maguire interrupts this beautiful soliloquy with, "Shut up. . . . You had me at 'Hello.'"

In other words, the moment they laid eyes on each other, he captured her heart. Their hearts were knit together again as they reconciled with each other. The mistakes that became obstacles were overcome by their love for one another. The movie ends with Jerry Maguire making the necessary changes to make her his priority. "You had me at 'Hello'" has stayed with us ever since, because everyone desires unconditional love.

When someone is "under the influence" of alcohol or drugs, that person is said to be controlled by a foreign substance. The power of the substance alters and impairs the decisions of the person under its influence. Well, there is another foreign substance that alters your decision-making. It is the most precious manifestation of the Holy Spirit: the love of God. This is the first influential substance that shapes our character that we will talk about in this chapter. God is love (see 1 John 4:16), and love is a substantive, powerful force.

Not only does love affect us, but it affects God as well. How did David have such an influence upon the heart of God, unlike other kings? David was a lovesick worshiper who learned to gaze upon the beauty of the Lord (see Psalm 27:4). More than simply participating in worship events, David lived a lifestyle of worshipful obedience. As a matter of fact, David's situation with Absalom turned when he went to a mountain summit "where people used to worship God" (2 Samuel 15:32). In that place, apparently moments after David prayed, God sent Hushai to meet David and, consequently, to thwart the counsel of Ahithophel (see 2 Samuel 15:31–37). David was a man after God's own heart (see 1 Samuel 13:14) because he was under the influence of God's love for him. Even in his weaknesses and failings, David endeavored to pursue right relationship with God (see 2 Samuel 12:13–22; Psalm 51).

In similar manner, people under the influence of love will alter their life decisions in order to sustain and maintain that relationship. Influence is obtained through intimacy and grows by relationship. Surprisingly to some, it is the same in our relationship with God in prayer and intercession. David's occupation was king, but his preoccupation was God.

Arresting Affections

By definition, influence addresses the effect a person has on the decisions of another. The spiritual force of influence affects the heart and soul of the recipient. The key word here is *affect*, which makes up the word *affection*. Influence at its core is about capturing the affections of another. Thoughts, decisions and outcomes are altered and determined as a result. The degree to which a person has intimately gripped the heart of another will determine the depth of influence that person can exert over the other.

The world system, which is controlled by the kingdom of darkness, seeks to accomplish this with media ads full of sexual innuendo. The reason marketers use sex to sell is that—well—it works! It works because it momentarily simulates the gripping effects that a transparent, intimate and loving relationship has upon us. In thirty seconds, advertisers use sexual images or inferences to create an emotion, then attach

> Influence at its core is about capturing the affections of another. Thoughts, decisions and outcomes are altered and determined as a result. The degree to which a person has intimately gripped the heart of another will determine the depth of influence that person can exert over the other.

the name of their product to that feeling. The suggestion is that if you want this feeling, then you must buy this product.

What are the relationship dynamics of influence released through God's Kingdom in prayer, and how do they work? Can God be arm-twisted and manipulated into doing what we want? Of course not, but these questions and others will be addressed as you read. Intimacy is more than a formula, and you will see how it results in influence with our Creator through prayer. It is one thing to shout Bible promises in prayer, but it is another thing altogether to whisper into the ear of the King of all creation and move His heart. We will explore this as we relate to God as Bridegroom, Friend and Father. First, let's look at the reciprocal effects of influence in human relationships.

When a man and woman begin dating, their friends are usually amazed at the attention the couple gives one another. If someone asks about going somewhere or doing something with those in "couplehood," the pair will usually confer with each other first before making a decision. "Da fellas" usually grow frustrated when their friend says, "Well, let me wait to check with my sweetheart before I say yes or no in case she has something planned for us that day." This progresses to "Let me check with her to see what she thinks about this or that." The beauty is that, well into marriage, solid couples still do this. Why? Because their spouses have so arrested their affections that there are few places they want to go without them. There is nothing the husbands want to do without their wives' input, and vice versa. Their hearts have been so captured by each other that their decision-making has been affected.

This happens because they spend quality time together. As a consequence, they even acquire each other's mental and spiritual attributes. Even some of the logic, manner of speech, actions and characteristics are similar because of the quality time they spend with one another.

Because solid husbands and wives desire to please each other and yearn to be with one another, they prioritize their relationship above all other human relationships. They have set forth principles to live by so that no person or thing can compromise their relationship. They share the same likes and dislikes. As a result, their decision-making has been affected. This is all because these couples are under the influence of each other's love. To understand the influence we have with God, we must understand the mutuality of influence. This determines whether a relationship is impersonal or interpersonal.

In regard to our human relationships, God has created us to receive and exert influence upon one another. Any relationship where one person exerts influence upon another person but does not allow the other person to influence him or her in return is an impersonal relationship. An extreme example is a slave or servant relationship. The slave has no input. That person is robbed of personhood because his or her only form of communication is the monologue of the dominant person. On the other hand, an interpersonal relationship is any relationship where both parties willfully open up to being influenced by each other. They both see the benefit of each other's mutual input. As a result, there is a dialogue.

Think about this: God allows *us* to influence *Him* through prayer. Of course, God cannot be manipulated or coerced; and, conversely, He respects our personhood in similar manner by knocking on rather than kicking open the door to our hearts (see Revelation 3:20). Our relationship with Him is not impersonal, but interpersonal. Prayer is a dialogue rather than a monologue. And to a greater measure than we know or can even imagine, God limits His involvement on earth to our connection with Him through prayer and intercession (see Ezekiel 22:30–31; Amos 3:7). Though He could do everything without us, many times He chooses to need us.

God graciously empowers us with the ability to influence Him through prayer and to affect what happens on earth. As we have seen, in order to influence another person, you must be able to arrest the affections of the other person and capture his or her heart. So the question is, Can you capture the heart of God? And the answer is yes, you can.

Arresting Our King's Affections

Not only are our affections arrested by God's love, but we can arrest His affections by our love as well. The ability to grip God's heart in this manner can be seen through the types and shadows of Christ our Bridegroom King and His Bride, the Church, in Song of Songs 4:9. In this passage, the Bridegroom King says to His Bride, "You have *stolen my heart*, my sister, my bride; you have *stolen my heart* with one glance of your eyes, with one jewel of your necklace" (emphasis added). The English phrase "stolen my heart" translates the Hebrew word *labab*, which comes from the Hebrew word *leb* ("heart"), but *labab* conveys so much more.

In other versions, this word is translated as "ravished my heart," "captured my heart" or "made my heart beat faster." It is interesting how many English words translators use to explain the one Hebrew word *labab*. There is not one English word that can convey the full meaning of this word, so they must use several English words to aid their description. *Strong's Concordance* says that *labab* means "to unheart [in a good sense] or to transport [with love]." *Unheart* is not even a word, but Strong chose to use "to unheart" to convey the meaning of *labab*!

The Hebrew understanding of *labab* is that one's heart is captured and captivated by another person. His or her beating heart is so ravished that it is "opened up" or "unhearted" in order to grant access to the one he or she desires. It has surrendered access to the one who has become the object of affection. His or her heart is openly shared with the other person. Listen: God chose this word to describe the passion Jesus our King has for us. Incredible! With just one glimpse of your eyes toward Him, you have captured His heart and made it beat faster.

The fact that Christ is trying to catch a glimpse means that He is staring. A man or woman who is attracted to someone will stare across the room without end just to make eye contact. You have seen it in love stories or done it before yourself. You longingly watch forever, it seems. Then, finally, the moment you have waited for comes. The brushing off of others and setting aside of all distractions has paid off, because the other person is looking your way. Suddenly, you make eye contact. Your stare meets his or her receptive glimpse, and the extended wait is all worth it, as your heart is beating with joy.

Did you know that Christ stares at you with the same fervent anticipation of your turning in His direction? He literally set aside every hindrance, including sin, Satan and other distractions, just to peer at you. You have so ravished His heart that He would rather die than spend eternity without you, which is exactly what He demonstrated in His death on the cross. You are that much of a priority to Him. His desire is a face-to-face encounter with you. And when you glimpse Him in prayer and worship, His heart beats faster.

One day in prayer, as I was meditating on Song of Songs 4:9, I felt the love of Christ in a powerful and moving way. As I was praying, I heard the Lord say, *William, if a mere glimpse has that kind of effect on My heart, imagine what happens when My Bride gazes at Me.* I began to weep uncontrollably. Think of it: If God stares longingly at you for a momentary glimpse that makes His heart beat faster, what if you gaze at Him? Imagine the effect your gaze can have upon His heart. He will not be able to contain Himself, and neither will you! Don't wait until you feel bad enough to come into His presence or have tried to clean yourself up. He just wants you to confess your faults and ask for forgiveness so that everything that hinders love can be removed. Honestly, you had Him at "Hello" (see Luke 15:17–24).

And He does not want to settle for a momentary glimpse; He wants your worship, He wants your gaze. Sometimes you gaze at your problems and only glimpse at the Lord for the answers! You have gazed at people, problems, failures and fears long enough. God blesses intimacy with Him and rewards us with Himself and everything else pertaining to life and godliness (see Hebrews 11:6; 2 Peter 1:3). Problems are changed in His presence.

There is no desire to twist God's arm or manipulate Him in this place of intimacy, because His desires have now become yours, and His will becomes your agenda in prayer. "Thy Kingdom come. Thy will be done" takes on a whole new meaning as you set aside your dominion for His. Again, God cannot be manipulated or coerced, but when we seek first His Kingdom, everything else is added, and He takes care of our needs (see Matthew 6:33).

If you gaze at Him and come under the influence of His love for you, you will be changed from being in His presence. Intimacy with Him affects His heart as well as yours. God knows you so well that you will notice Him finishing your sentences, because you are communicating from thought to thought. Instead of only seeing His acts, you will understand His ways (see Psalm 103:7). The Bible will become your "love language" of communication with God in prayer. He may even give you a "prayer language" to share with Him, and those around you will not understand what you say, because this talk is spiritually appraised (see 1 Corinthians 2:14; 12:10–11; 14:39–40).

As a consequence, when God has become your priority, there will be a set of principles you will desire to live by in order to maintain your relationship. Why? Since God is your first love, you make Him first place in your life (see Matthew 22:37). Before you say yes to anything else, you will check with God and do what He desires. So that your relationship is not compromised, there will be things you stop doing, places you will not go and people you will no longer desire to be around. You have placed God above every relationship (spouse, family, friends, etc.). You see, your decisions are affected, and your life is no longer the way it used to be when you are under the influence of God's love for you. His love will compel and constrain you (see Ezekiel 36:26–27).

The beauty is that what you behold is what you become. From spending quality time together, you will acquire God's attributes and characteristics. You will love what He loves and hate what He hates. The end result is that you are shaped into His image and likeness. Spiritual osmosis takes place. Genesis 1:26 says, "Then God said, 'Let Us make man in Our image, according to Our likeness'" (NASB). You are conformed to His image and become a transformed representative (see Romans 8:29; 12:2).

Also, your lifestyle of worship and adoration will attract others to Him. "God said to them, 'Be fruitful and multiply, and fill the earth, and subdue it; and rule over . . .'" (Genesis 1:28 NASB). As Francis Frangipane says, the principle is that once we become like Him, He multiplies us. Godly influence on earth does not come from seeking crowds but rather is a byproduct of seeking God. You attract people to God when they see your passion for the object of your gaze. He has become the object of your utmost affection. You in turn introduce them to your Lord, whose cross has changed your life.

So how does God share His heart with us, and how do we gaze at the Lord? You gaze by spending time in praise and worship, as you open your heart to God. You gaze by spending time in the Bible, which is your mirror that aligns your heart to God's heart. You gaze by spending time in fasting and prayer, where your heart is enlarged by God. All of these, joined with the crucible of life's circumstances, conform you into God's image, creating a lifestyle of worship.

Through prayer and a lifestyle of worship, then, you can step into a place of intimacy with God so powerful that it will affect others around you. When you allow God to capture your heart, He will give you His influence. It will flow through your passion and transform everyone around you. When the bride described her bridegroom to her friends in Song of Songs 5:10–16, their reply was, "Which way did your lover turn, that we may look for him with you?" (6:1). Her description of the one she loved was so powerful that it affected everyone with whom she came in contact. This happened because she was lovesick (see 5:8).

Remember, *influence* used to be understood as a contagious infection. In similar manner, as we see in the Song of Songs, people of godly influence possess epidemic adoration. Infused with God's love, their passion is contagious and affects everyone around them. The same can be true of your relationship with God. When you are under the influence of His love, others will be attracted. What an awesome byproduct of intimacy! We relate to God not only as a Bride through prayer, however, but also as His friends.

No Greater Love

Seeing the words *friend* and *God* in the same sentence seems sacrilegious to some people. Their extreme focus on the fear of God leaves no room for friendship. And others denigrate the revelation of God as friend by treating it with a familiarity that depreciates this reality. Nonetheless, the truth is that our Lord, the King of all creation, does have a desire for our friendship. He is our majestic friend who sticks closer than a brother, who shares His heart and history with us. God chose to use the friendship of David and Jonathan as an example of the influence we can have with Him as a covenant friend.

Again, a major aspect of influence is the ability to arrest the affections or capture the heart of another person so powerfully that it affects the outcome of his or her choices. David and Jonathan were friends who definitely captured each other's hearts to this degree. "The soul of Jonathan was knit to the soul of David, and Jonathan loved him as himself" (1 Samuel 18:1 NASB). Their hearts were "*labab*-ed": transported, unhearted and knit together. *Labab* is about not only romantic love, but also covenant love and devotion. David and Jonathan were spiritual brothers whose covenantal relationship transcended classism and nepotism. Though David was Saul's servant, David and Jonathan fought for one another. Instead of contending for Saul, his father, Jonathan contended for David, his father's replacement. While Saul was king of Israel, Jonathan disclosed to David everything his father was trying to do to kill him.

Though Jonathan was the son of a king, and David was a lowly shepherd and servant, their relationship was not impersonal. They enjoyed mutual respect for one another. They had an interpersonal relationship, and there was a reciprocal influence from one to the other. The Bible says they loved each other as they loved their own lives (see 1 Samuel 18:1; 20:17). This was by no means a romantic love, but a spiritual kindredness shared between two covenant brothers who knew they were connected beyond life. Spiritual osmosis created a likeness in their character, values and love for God. They made a covenant together, and David agreed to honor their covenant even beyond Jonathan's life.

The first act of a new king was to kill anyone who was part of the former regime. Anticipating the day when David would become king, Jonathan asked David, "If I am still alive, will you not show me the lovingkindness of the LORD, that I may not die?" (1 Samuel 20:14 NASB). David promised Jonathan he would not kill him or his family when he became king. Jonathan also said, "You shall not cut off your lovingkindness from my house forever" (1 Samuel 20:15 NASB). Jonathan's request was that this covenant be extended to his household, or offspring, in future generations.

David did finally become king of Israel, but his friend Jonathan died before then. Later on, after David's reign was well established, David remembered the covenant love and devotion of his friend who was closer than a brother. He asked, "Is there anyone still left of the house of Saul to whom I can show kindness for Jonathan's sake?" (2 Samuel 9:1). Later he rephrased his question, saying, "Is there no one still left of the house of Saul to whom I can show God's kindness?" (2 Samuel 9:3).

David was revealing the kindness of God to us. Mephibosheth, Jonathan's crippled son, was brought out of fear and hiding to live in David's palace. Mephibosheth knew nothing of David's covenant with Jonathan, but his life was affected because King David was still under the influence of his covenant friend, Jonathan. Isn't that incredible? Jonathan's son became King David's son and lived in his palace. King David's choices for an entire family were influenced by one man for generations. David even extended the covenant to Mephibosheth's offspring.

The mind-blowing concept was that David said this was "God's kindness." If this human relationship was meant to reveal what God's kindness is like, then it means there is the ability not only to capture His heart, as we saw previously, but also to have our hearts knit to His. This happens when we move into covenant relationship. King David was revealing to us the desire of the King of kings, Jesus Christ. Through King Jesus' covenant love displayed on the cross, we can enter into His suffering and resurrection power when we covenant with the Friend who sticks closer than a brother (see Proverbs 18:24).

Jesus said, in John 15:13, "Greater love has no one than this, that one lay down his life for his friends" (NASB). This is what He did for us, and when we lay down our lives for Him, we move to a deeper place of intimate friendship. Jesus went on to say, "No longer do I call you slaves, for the slave does not know what his master is doing; but I have called you friends, for all things that I have heard from My Father I have made known to you" (John 15:15 NASB).

From Slave to Friend

There is a mutual receptivity of influence with God as a friend; a slave does not know what the master is doing, but a friend does. Slavery is an impersonal relationship, but friendship is interpersonal. Just as Jonathan told David the plans his father had for him, Jesus our Lord and Friend will make known to us all things the Father has made known to Him. And unlike Saul's plans, the plans the Father has for us are good (see Jeremiah 29:11)! He will also show us great and unsearchable things that we do not know (see Jeremiah 33:3). When we are His friends, He reveals to us good and bad things, previously unknown to us, so that we can partner with Him in intercessory prayer.

Consider the example of the apostle John. As "the disciple whom Jesus loved," he had such an intimate friendship with Christ that the other disciples asked him for inside information (see John 13:22–25). This "friend" was indeed informed of things he did not know, being given the book of Revelation to share with the rest of the world. In laying down His life, Jesus also entrusted John with one of Jesus' most valuable earthly treasures: His mother (see John 19:26–27). This happened because Jesus' and John's hearts were knit together in covenant.

In Jesus' friendship with Mary and Martha, we see intimacy and influence at work as the women pleaded for their brother.

We also see the difference between favor and influence. Martha and Mary both had favor that granted them access to Jesus. In Luke 10:38–42, however, we see how both of them were near the Lord, but only one of them was actually *with* the Lord. Martha had a servant mentality and was consumed with how she served; Mary was a friend and was consumed with *whom* she served.

When their brother, Lazarus, died, we see the individual impact each sister had upon Jesus, though He loved them both. In this instance, they both had favor, but only one had influence. They both said the same words to Jesus: "Lord, if you had been here, my brother would not have died" (John 11:21, 32). Jesus' response to Martha was a teaching about the resurrection. But Mary's tearful plea invoked a response from the Lord that allowed her to see that His heart was visibly moved: Jesus wept (see John 11:35). Jesus and Mary wept together because their hearts were knit together; they were friends, and He felt what she felt. Martha saw God's acts, but Mary experienced God's heart and knew His ways (see Psalm 103:7). Martha's favor obtained her revelation about the resurrection, but Mary's brokenness resulted in influence that raised her brother from the dead.

What I want you to see is that there is a place of friendship with Christ where your heart can be knit together with His, but it comes when you lay down your life in covenant. He is still looking for friends to whom He can entrust His precious possessions. Do not just assume that this is reserved for other people. God desires this level of intimacy with *you*. While you are busy saying, *I know John and Mary had deep, affectionate relationships with the Lord back then, but I want it now. Why not me?* the Lord is saying, *Why not you?* God desires to have a relationship like this with you.

Because He is the same yesterday, today and forever, God still responds to our intercession on behalf of our loved ones and friends, as you will see in the following incredible testimony from a dear brother who asked for anonymity. As you read, you will see that this in no way hinders the credibility of this remarkable account—but actually enhances it. You see, my friend is so greatly under the influence of Christ's love that he wants to make sure God is the One who receives glory for this amazing story. What a star!

While on a ministry trip, I dreamed I came across a boy who had died just seconds before I saw him. Around him were rescue workers who tried to no avail to bring him back. The moment I laid eyes on him, I was convicted that it was not supposed to be this way. Following that conviction, I prayed. The only words that came forth were, "Life and healing in Jesus' name." The little boy in the dream came back to life, and the dream ended. The following morning, the Holy Spirit reminded me of this dream, and as I shared this with some friends they thought it was symbolic; but something inside me was not settled with that answer.

That same day, I was walking along a four-lane thoroughfare with a good friend who is from Australia. We were walking across the street, when I paused to put something in my car. My friend went on ahead. Because he looks for cars coming from the opposite direction in his country, he did not see a car traveling forty miles per hour on our side of the road—and it struck him. There was no warning, just the blunt sound of the impact when the car hurled my friend more than thirty feet. As I watched him flying through the air, the Lord prompted my heart, *This is your dream.*

I immediately ran up to my friend and found him in the same position as the boy in my dream. I checked for his pulse, having been trained in CPR, and found none. Without any hesitation, I began to pray as in my dream, "Life and healing in Jesus' name." My prayers quickly rose to shouts of desperation: *Life and healing in Jesus' name!* Moments later, my friend suddenly gasped for a breath of air and rolled onto his back. Though now with a pulse, his broken body was pouring so much blood that it ran off the asphalt and pooled along the side of the street. The worst of these injuries were from his skull.

As I continued praying, I watched the Lord work as the blood that was flowing from his head simply stopped. The Lord continued healing, and by the time my friend was placed in the ambulance, he said his name! He became so coherent that he actually prayed for us while he was in the ambulance. When he made it to the hospital, doctors ran test after test and were astonished because they could not believe he sustained such an impact and injuries and yet was still alive!

Today my friend is healed, and he travels, ministering the Gospel. We've shared this story, and God is using it to change lives and resurrect hopes and dreams wherever we go.

Incredible! The enemy's plans were thwarted because God made my brother in Christ aware of "great things he knew not of" in a dream—and he responded with prayer. Yes, God still has influence over death and our destinies and allows us to partner with Him in intercession for others.

Generational Influence

And as we have observed, God's kindness revealed through David and Jonathan's relationship demonstrates that we can have influence with God through prayer that affects future generations. If King David remembered his covenant with Jonathan and blessed his friend's future generations, how much more will the King of Glory? In other words, as friends of King Jesus, we can move His heart for generations to come.

God honors the legacy of His covenant friends. Exodus 20:5–6 speaks of generational curses and blessings. Generational curses extend to three or four generations, but God said He will show generational blessings "to a thousand generations of those who love me and keep my commandments"—which means, basically, forever. You can be a friend of God and shape history for generations. Can you imagine how thankful Mephibosheth must have been for his father, Jonathan's, intercession and for King David's generosity? I can. Let me explain.

In *History Makers* (Regal, 2004), which I co-authored with Dutch Sheets, I talk about an heirloom that has been passed down for generations in my family: a cast-iron kettle that is now more than two hundred years old. While it was used for cooking, it was also secretly used for prayer by my forefathers, who were Christian slaves on a plantation in Lake Providence, Louisiana. Forbidden to pray and beaten severely if caught doing so, they gathered in a barn to have secret prayer meetings. They laid down their lives in order to spend quality time with God in prayer. On earth they had a master who was a tyrant, but in prayer they had a Master who was a Friend.

In spite of the danger, they would sneak into a barn late at night, doing all they could to make sure their prayer meeting went unnoticed. As they carefully opened the door, they eased into the barn, carrying this black kettle. Once inside, they turned the kettle upside down on the dirt floor of the barn and placed three or four rocks under the rim to prop up the kettle and create an opening. Then they lay prostrate on the ground around the kettle, with their mouths close to the opening. You see, the kettle muffled their voices as they prayed through the night.

Revelation 5:8 speaks of "bowls full of incense, which are the prayers of the saints" before the throne of God. Revelation 8:3–5 shows that at some point—in the future, no doubt, when God realizes the time is right—He adds His incense and fire to these prayers and throws them to earth in the form of judgments and power. My family's kettle literally became a bowl of intercession.

One of my ancestors, who was present at these prayer meetings as a young girl, passed down the following information along with the kettle: "These slaves were not praying for their freedom at all. They did not think they would see freedom in their time, so they prayed for the freedom of their children and their children's children." That absolutely amazes me. These friends of God risked their lives to pray for the freedom of their children and the ensuing generations! Like Jonathan, they did not live to see the promise, but they laid a foundation through intercession that affected future generations.

One day liberation did come. While many of those who prayed did not live to see freedom, their prayers were answered. The young girl who passed down these stories attended these prayer meetings until slavery was abolished. As a teenager, she was set free from slavery. Can you imagine being one whom freedom fell upon, having for many years listened to others pray for your freedom?

Unfortunately, no one alive today knows her name. I believe this nameless teenage girl saw fit to pass down this kettle because she knew that not only was she standing on the sacrifice of others' devotion to Christ, but so was everyone born after her in her family. She was careful to preserve and pass on both the kettle and its history. She passed it to her daughter, Harriet Locket, who passed it to Nora Locket, who passed it to William Ford Sr., who passed it to William Ford Jr., who gave it to me, William Ford III.

God passed along not only a kettle as an inheritance, however. He passed on a spiritual inheritance and generational blessings into our lives as well. God answered not only my predecessors' prayers for national freedom but also their intercessions for spiritual freedom in our family. You see, God found a "Mephibosheth" like me because of their covenant devotion to Christ. And not just me but most of my family members are saved and following Christ as a result of God answering prayers offered up to Him long ago. Generational blessings have overtaken us because two hundred years ago our forefathers laid down their lives in prayer and became friends of God. It amazes me that the Lord has been under the influence of their devotion ever since. This was all accomplished by God empowering that generation with the ability to grip His heart. My prayer is that you and I can be graced to do the same so that future generations even yet to be created may praise the Lord.

The Father Loves You

We relate to God not only as friends in this manner but also as sons and daughters of Father God. Likewise, in my relationship with my parents, growing up and still today, there are things I will not do and places I will not go because of their influence in my life. I have opened my heart to their wisdom, knowledge and years of experience—not because we have the same biological makeup but because of the love they have demonstrated toward me. As a result, I share my heart with them on decisions I want to make. There are many things even today that I will not initiate without conferring with my parents, as well as with other spiritual mothers and fathers. And as I have matured and grown, my parents in turn have opened their hearts to receive my input on business, family and relationship decisions in their lives. We both have benefited from a mutual respect and reciprocal influence because our hearts are gripped together in love.

Jesus modeled this same type of mutual respect and influence with His Father in heaven. He clearly indicated that He did not do anything by His own initiative but rather did only what He saw His Father doing (see John 8:28). Jesus did only what His Father desired because He was influenced by His Father's love for Him. The Father had allowed Himself to be open to the Son's influence and input upon Creation, as all things were created by and for Christ (see Colossians 1:16). As Jesus matured in His tenure on earth, the Father was so influenced by the Son that

He allowed Him to shape the affairs of humankind in the family business of redeeming lost humanity. Because of the joy set before Him, and under the influence of the Father's love, Christ achieved His desire of pleasing His Father and returning back into His presence, thus securing our salvation.

When apprehended by His enemies, Jesus had enough influence to call down twelve legions of angels but instead submitted Himself to the Father's will to go to the cross. Christ was so confident of His Father's affection for Him that He went to the cross trusting and knowing that His Father was able to raise Him up again—and He did. Hebrews 5:7 says that Jesus offered up prayers and was heard because of His obedience. In other words, His prayers were not lip service. His prayers were matched with a heart fully submitted to the Father's will and a lifestyle of worship. This is what moved God to listen and act upon His requests. Because of His prayers and obedience to go to the cross, it was the Father's good pleasure not only to give Him the Kingdom but also to answer His request and give Him the nations (you and me) as His inheritance (see Psalm 2:8).

Being friends of the King, we are now also family members— joint heirs with Christ—and it is the Father's good pleasure to give us the Kingdom as well (see Luke 12:32). Just as David remembered Jonathan's devotion, Father God remembers the devotion of His Son, who laid down His life for His friends. And when we have an intimate relationship with Jesus, using His name in prayer has influence, because the Father is still affected by the sacrificial devotion of His Son.

Void of a relationship with Christ, however, use of His name carries no weight. Consider the sons of Sceva, who tried to cast out demons using Jesus' name but had no influence because they had no relationship with Christ (see Acts 19:13–16). Jesus told His disciples, "In that day you will ask in My name, and I do not say to you that I will request of the Father on your behalf; for the Father Himself loves you, because you have loved Me and have believed that I came forth from the Father" (John 16:26–27 NASB). "In the name of Jesus" has influence only when we are in a loving relationship with Christ.

Don't miss Jesus' amazing statement here: "The Father Himself loves you, because you have loved Me and have believed that I came forth from the Father." Do you love Jesus? Do you believe that He came forth from the Father? If the answer to both of these questions is yes, know that what Jesus says is true. Father God Himself loves you, just as He loves Jesus (see John 17:23). This is why He sent His Son to rescue you from hell and enable you to reign with Him. Father God loves you, and He allows you to influence through prayer not only what happens in your own life but also the lives and destinies of others—and even nations.

> Father God loves you, and He allows you to influence through prayer not only what happens in your own life but also the lives and destinies of others— and even nations.

Because we are sons and daughters of God, when we grow in intimacy and maturity in our relationship with Him, He will increase our sphere of authority and empower it with His influence. There is a place in intimacy with Father God where we move beyond praying our list and shouting Scripture promises to Him: a place where He shares His heart with us and allows us to influence Him and what happens in history. We see this in Genesis 18:17, as God says, "Shall I hide from Abraham what I am about to do?" God would not do anything to Sodom and Gomorrah without informing Abraham, who had an interpersonal relationship with God and was involved in an intercessory dialogue with the Father (see verses 18–33).

What kind of influence will your prayer life have on future generations? Think of how many Mephibosheths could be affected by your prayers! Open your heart to the King of Glory, and knit yourself to Him in covenant love. Let God arrest your affections. Fix your gaze on the author and finisher of your history. There is a prayer bowl over your family, neighborhood, city and nation. You, too, can move to a place of influence with God that affects the destinies of others, even nations, through prayer.

And when you are under the influence of Christ's love, your doubts are obliterated. This is why the character quality we will discuss in the next chapter is faith, the substance of things hoped for (see Hebrews 11:1).

EXERCISING INFLUENCE *through Prayer*

Father, I thank You that because of Your love, rather than spending eternity without me, Your Son chose to die on a cross for my sins. You then raised Him up, that I may be saved by His life. O Lord, I respond to this love by laying down my life and surrendering my heart to You. Empower me to move from a glimpse to a gaze in our relationship, until my heart beats faster with Yours. Arrest my affections, knit our hearts together, until I am completely under the influence of Your love.

You are my priority, and I place You above every relationship in my life. I want Your love to forever influence my thinking and decision-making. May Your influence in my life even reach generations to come!

Your kindness not only knits our hearts together, it also leads people to repentance. So, God, I ask You to tip the prayer bowls over our nations and rescue a generation of needy souls who, like Mephibosheth, are fatherless and broken and do not know that the King's desire for them is good. Raise up lovesick warriors in the Church whose epidemic adoration will create a spiritual pandemic.

Finally, may Your heart beat faster with these words: Father God, I love and adore You! Even more, be moved by these words: In Jesus' name. Amen.

4

Rhyme, Reason
and the Substance
of Faith

I KNOW YOU HAVE BEEN READING for a while, so let's participate in a little exercise just to keep you sharp. Here are the instructions. I am going to give you a word to say, and I want you to repeat it out loud ten times. Then I want you to answer a simple question before looking at the next page.

The word is *F-o-l-k*. Say it out loud ten times, then quickly answer the question that immediately follows. Ready?

"Folk." "Folk." "Folk." "Folk." "Folk." "Folk." "Folk." "Folk." "Folk." "Folk."

Question: What do you call the white part of an egg?

"Yolk" was probably your first-impulse answer; the correct answer, however, is "egg white." Yolk is the *yellow* part, remember?

Tell me the truth: You said "yolk," didn't you! Maybe you did not say it, but if you are like most people, you at least had the inclination to say "yolk." Normally, I do this exercise in churches and conferences with hundreds, sometimes thousands, of people in the audience, and I have everyone say the answer at the same time. Imagine this exercise under those conditions, with a multitude of voices shouting the wrong answer in unison. Honestly, it is rather amusing!

Sometimes I have to ask the question three or four times before I get the correct answer from the entire group. Why? Because of the influence of the reasoning or logic set in place through repetition. This is coupled with the time constraint of a quick response, which creates an impulsive answer; so the first "logical" answer is one that rhymes.

The other major factor that affects the answer is social influence. Many times our responses are conditioned by the people around us. Most people do not like being the only one giving a different answer, especially when it is repeated over and over again. So they put their trust in what others are saying and go along with whatever seems socially acceptable—even if it is wrong. You may be thinking, *Okay, Ford, so what does this have to do with godly influence and faith?* And my answer is, *Everything!*

Consider the debate on "the separation of church and state," for example. The original intent of this phrase was to create religious freedom, not religious oppression—as it is so often interpreted today. Most people have been led to believe that the separation of church and state is mentioned in our constitution, but it is not. It was not even written in a legal document but rather in a letter by Thomas Jefferson ensuring a Baptist denomination that a wall of separation between the church and the state would not occur.

The idea was to protect the freedom *of* religion, not the freedom *from* religion, as it is currently defined. Yet because history revisionists repeatedly have perpetuated the persistent lie that separation of church and state means freedom from religion, phrases like *under God* and historical documents such as the Ten Commandments have been threatened to be removed from government buildings. This influence, of course, comes from the evil one, who desires to remove the history of God's faithfulness from our nation. God is calling us now to speak the truth in love and contend in prayer and intercession for our faith and heritage.

Influential Faith

The next influential substance we will discuss is faith. One of the impartations of the Holy Spirit is the gift of faith, of which every person has a measure (see Romans 12:3). In this chapter, we will talk about faith and the importance of the company we keep. You will also see how the depth of your conviction creates the character necessary to have godly influence in prayer. Giant strongholds can come down through people of faith.

Influence is a substance, and so is faith, according to the Bible. Hebrews 11:1 says, "Now faith is the *substance* of things hoped for, the *evidence* of things not seen" (KJV, emphasis added). People who have godly influence are people of faith, and they are able to grip God's heart in ways that doubtful people cannot. Why? Because faith pleases God (see Hebrews 10:38; 11:6). One person with the gift of faith can change the atmosphere of a room, even a nation. David demonstrated this kind of influential faith when he faced the Philistine champion, Goliath.

There was more going on behind the scenes, in the spiritual realm, with Goliath and David's confrontation. Goliath was more than a giant. He was representing a major, dark, territorial spirit. He was a spokesman for the kingdom of darkness and was no doubt infused with the power and influence of the Philistines' false god Dagon (see 1 Samuel 5:1–3). The Israelites were paralyzed by Goliath's size, taunts and dark influence, and the atmosphere of the battleground was lethal, having depleted Israel's faith in God over the past forty days (see 1 Samuel 17:16). But David, who was not conditioned by the influence of the environment of the battleground, ran into the fight. He rehearsed his history with God instead of rehearsing the enemy's taunts. He basically said, "By the power of God, I killed a lion, I killed a bear and, with God, I can take Goliath, too!" (see 1 Samuel 17:34–37). David, a mere shepherd boy, defeated Goliath by his faith in God, which gripped God's heart. David was *God's* spokesman, infused with *His* power.

In the natural, David accomplished Goliath's defeat by striking him with one stone that sank into his forehead (see 1 Samuel 17:49). Goliath's forehead symbolized his thinking, reasoning and mindset. So spiritually, this defeat represents the breaking of the mind control and false ideologies of Dagon. As a result, God released His power through David, and the fearful grip the enemy had over Israel was shattered. David's faith was so powerful that when the strong man Goliath was conquered, so was the fearful, paralyzing influence Dagon had on Israel. After the Philistine champion's defeat, his comrades turned and ran, and the Israelites surged forward with a shout to defeat and plunder the enemy (see 1 Samuel 17:51–54).

Jesus said, "When a strong man, fully armed, guards his own palace, his goods are in peace. But when a stronger than he comes upon him and overcomes him, he takes from him all his armor in which he trusted, and divides his spoils" (Luke 11:21–22 NKJV). David was a spoiler whose faith in God took out a giant strong man and rallied his nation to victory.

Not only do we see the effects of one person's faith here, but this story also reveals how comments constantly spoken to us (especially negative comments) can influence our decision-making. Beyond the Israelites' listening to Goliath's taunts, they also kept rehearsing what the enemy was saying to them (see 1 Samuel 17:25). This atmosphere of doubt and unbelief was toxic, affecting everyone in the environment.

To be effective in prayer, we must be aware of the impact of negative words and attitudes coming from the people around us. These negative influences can be compared to the odorless, colorless, toxic gas carbon monoxide. It is impossible to see, taste or smell the poisonous fumes. Low levels of unknown exposure to it cause people to become sick with influenza-like symptoms. At higher levels, unknown exposure to carbon monoxide causes death if you stay in the environment long enough. Undetected, the influence of carbon monoxide is lethal.

In like manner, sustained negative influences of sin, doubt and unbelief are lethal to your faith. Proverbs 18:21 says, "The tongue has the power of life and death, and those who love it will eat its fruit." The word *power* in this verse is the Hebrew word *yad*, which can also be translated "influence." This verse could be rephrased, "The tongue has the *influence* of life and death." Words are seeds of influence, and what you sow is what you grow (see Galatians 6:7–8). The fruit or manifestation of your words are their negative or positive effects on the behavior of those around you.

One dictionary defines *influence* as "a spiritual force or moral force, which, knowingly or unknowingly, affects the actions and behaviors of others, consciously or unconsciously." So really, the question we must ask ourselves is not, "Am I being influenced?" but rather "What is influencing me?" In *Understanding the Purpose and Power of Prayer* (Whitaker House, 2002), Myles Munroe says, "Check what you're listening to and to whom you're listening; check the books you read, the music you listen to, the movies and videos you watch and the church you attend—because you will become what you listen to and speak what you hear."

This is why—in order to be people of influence in prayer—we must be around people who are imparting faith and encouragement to us. The company we keep has the ability to affect our attitude and actions, because faith comes by hearing. Unfortunately, doubt and unbelief come by hearing as well. Pessimistic thinking and discouraging words can be toxic and destroy your prayer life.

Proverbs 23:7 says, "For as he *thinks* in his heart, *so is he*" (NKJV, emphasis added). In other words, you become what you think about. And to a degree, you develop into the likeness of whoever put the thoughts into your mind. As you can see, over time the people around you begin to influence your attitude— what you believe, how you think—and you become like them. Another way to look at this proverb is to make it a question to yourself. "For as he thinks in his heart, so is he": *So am I negative? So am I pessimistic? So am I discouraged?*

Maybe the question you must ask yourself is "So am I under the influence of the company I keep?" Because of this, in certain seasons of your life, you must determine which people you are to disassociate from, which people you are to go to lunch with and which people you can go to war with! We need believers around us with the gift of faith to break the power of the fears that bind us. And that person is you. Like David, God wants you to influence the environment instead of the environment or circumstances influencing you.

Can I share with you a secret about my "folk" and "yolk" exercise? I have found that it takes only one person saying the right answer to spoil this exercise. With just one spoiler, this exercise will not work, even in a crowd with thousands of people. If the spoiler is wavering and says the correct answer doubtfully—"Umm, egg, uh, egg white?"—he or she will not have any influence on the others. But if the spoiler shouts the truth with conviction—"Egg white!"—everyone else will follow suit. The power is not in the volume but in the resolve. The spoiler may have to repeat the correct answer a few times, but eventually others will be speaking the truth, no longer bound by error.

> The depth of your conviction will determine the power of your influence.

No doubt you can see where I am going with this. Beloved, all God wants you to do, even when the crowd is in error, is have conviction, speak the truth in love and fight in intercession. Your faith will invoke God into the battle; He will fight for you, and through persistence the prevailing influence will change others. It is important to mention here that in the Hebrews 11:1 description of faith, the word *evidence* is also translated as "conviction" (NASB). You see, *the depth of your conviction will determine the power of your influence.* Like David, your stone of faith can be a weapon that shatters the paralyzing influence the enemy has on a nation and spoils the plans of the devil.

Becoming Intercession

Nehemiah was faced with a similar challenge. Many Israelites were under the influence of Sanballat and Tobiah and became afraid of their plot to overthrow the project of rebuilding Jerusalem's wall. Gripped by fear, these Israelites dreadfully reported the enemies' plan to their countrymen. Guess how many times they said it? Ten times, just like our exercise.

> When the Jews who lived near them came and told us ten times, "They will come up against us from every place where you may

turn," then I stationed men in the lowest parts of the space be-hind the wall, the exposed places, and I stationed the people in families with their swords, spears and bows. When I saw their fear, I rose and spoke to the nobles, the officials and the rest of the people: "Do not be afraid of them; remember the Lord who is great and awesome, and fight for your brothers, your sons, your daughters, your wives and your houses."

Nehemiah 4:12–14 NASB

Ten times the people were told that the enemy was coming, as their fellow Jews rehearsed and conveyed their message with great fear. From our exercise before, you can imagine the negative influence of this group and how fearful the masses became. Yet Nehemiah, by faith, interceded with truth and reminded Israel of God's power. He assured them that God is mighty to save. When Nehemiah called them to remembrance, he was basically saying, "Stop rehearsing what the enemy is saying, and rehearse the memory of God's faithfulness!"

The influence of Nehemiah's faith was so powerful that the people were willing to fight for their families. They prepared for battle and chose God's plan to rebuild instead of the enemy's plan of defeat. Nehemiah recalled, "When our enemies heard that we were aware of their plot and that God had frustrated it, we all returned to the wall, each to his own work. From that day on, half of my men did the work, while the other half were equipped with spears, shields, bows and armor" (Nehemiah 4:15–16).

When their adversaries heard of their faith, they canceled their assignment, and the Israelites finished the work. This hap-pened because Nehemiah, like David, used his stone of faith and hurled it at the intimidating influence of the enemy, and the enemy's plan was spoiled. Powerful! Our faith in God can take out the societal giants in our day. We must rise to the occasion and be spoilers as well.

It is not time to shrink back in fear, but rather it is time to stand in faith to rebuild the walls of our nation and fight for our sons, our daughters, our spouses and our homes. We must believe that when the enemy comes in like a flood, the Lord will lift up a standard against him (see Isaiah 59:18–19). Like those along the wall with Nehemiah, not only must we *do* intercession, but we must also *become* intercession by standing in the exposed places in society. We must stand in the gap for our families, communities and nation. We must put feet to our prayers, take our stand and face the opposing powers of our generation.

Churchill and Hitler

Winston Churchill demonstrated this at a critical juncture during World War II. Hitler's Germany, unbeknownst to many, was a nation gripped by the spiritual force granted to Adolf Hitler by demonic powers. Historians have revealed that Hitler sought influence from the kingdom of darkness through occult means. This, of course, explains not only his influence over the nation but also his brutal holocaust of the Jews. Hitler was a Goliath who spewed demonic ideologies of racism, hatred and death. Germany's army, a well-trained, formidable foe, was threatening total domination of Europe.

Gripped by dread, the people of Great Britain feared defeat by Germany because of casualties and key setbacks in the war. However, the conviction and resolve of Winston Churchill, the prime minister of England and a godly man, broke the power of Hitler's intimidating influence. Ironically, both of these men were used to influence the masses as masterful orators in their generation: one for evil, the other for good.

In his book *Never Give In: The Extraordinary Character of Winston Churchill* (Cumberland House, 1996), Stephen Mansfield observes that the primary issue of the war, for Churchill, was faith. Churchill was convinced that World War II was a battle between Christendom and Hitler's sinister paganism, and throughout the war, he replenished his extraordinary moral courage through prayer and worship. Churchill did not leave his faith in his prayer closet, nor did he leave it in the pew; rather he took it to the podium and changed the world.

On October 29, 1941, Churchill went to Harrow School to listen to the traditional songs he had sung there himself as a youth and to address the students. Although he spoke less than five minutes, this became one of his most famous and inspiring speeches. The following statement particularly infused England with hope and courage: "Never give in. Never give in. Never, never, never, never—in nothing, great or small, large or petty—never give in, except to convictions of honor and good sense. Never yield to force. Never yield to the apparently overwhelming might of the enemy."

The depth of Churchill's conviction in God released a powerful influence that obliterated doubts and shattered Hitler's spellbinding influence. As a result of England's renewed faith, the momentum of the war shifted. Because of the godly influence of Winston Churchill, the Allied forces won the war.

As you can see, Churchill's influence broke the spell of Hitler's intimidation and spoiled his plans for world domination. Powerful! You, too, can have the same influence in your walk with God. But how is it obtained? You must become a person who lives out his or her principles. Your convictions and principles will be motivated by God's love when your relationship with Him has become your priority. When this happens, you will love what He loves and hate what He hates. Then you will have basic biblical convictions that cannot be diluted by acceptance or compromise. Neither can you give in because of someone else's threats.

God is not attracted to or fooled by people who only talk the talk. He responds to praying people who uncompromisingly act on what they believe and are obedient (see Hebrews 5:7). To be a godly influence, therefore, you must meet this requirement. You must have conviction and be a person of principle, unlike others who compromise and are people of preference.

You must have a resolve that says, "God's Word is my standard, and I won't deviate from it." Regardless of the price, people of principle will not walk away from their convictions. They may be rejected; it may cost them their jobs, livelihoods, even their lives, but they will not alter or waver from their basic biblical convictions. A person of principle says, for example: "'Whatever a man sows, that he will also reap,' from Galatians 6:7–8, is a biblical principle. It can work for your benefit or your detriment, but you can't change it." A person of preference might say, "'Whatever a man sows, that he will also reap'— well, sometimes that's true," or in a particular instance, "That Scripture doesn't apply to me." A preference is something you believe under certain circumstances, something that can be twisted to fit what you desire in a given situation. In order to be a godly influence, what you believe must be aligned with how you live.

Rhyme—but Not Reason

Like Nehemiah, one person with godly influence must take a stand and speak the truth and remind others of who God is, even when false popular opinion is saying something quite different. As we saw in the "folk" and "yolk" exercise, many times the crowd may have the rhyme but not the reason (or more accurately, not the reasoning—meaning "right way of thinking"). They impulsively give an easy answer and stick with it because of everyone else's response.

society, for example, are trying to say that civil
gay rights are the same. Just like with "folk" and
have here a rhyme but with wrong reasoning. Civil
rights is about racial and gender equality that seeks justice
and fairness for all. Gay rights is really about endorsing homosexuality, which God clearly says is a sinful, forbidden
practice—along with all sex outside of heterosexual marriage
(see Romans 1:21–27; 1 Corinthians 6:9). Gay rights is about
a sexual behavior preference, while the civil rights movement
is about the principle of being given access in society on the
basis of character content rather than skin color or gender. The
reality of being born into a certain family and race cannot be
changed, but sexual behaviors and partners can be changed.
The truth is that the civil rights movement is about principles
and the gay rights movement is about preferences—they are
not equivalent.

The enemy has tried to use a twisted system of logic to hijack
a movement full of the blood of Christian martyrs. Under the
enemy's influence, homosexual pro-
testers have even sung civil rights bal-
lads such as "We Shall Overcome" in
order to attach themselves to the civil
rights movement. Sadly, this influence
has caused activist judges to pass rul-
ings to recognize same-sex marriages.
As many African-American pastors
have said, "The devil cannot use my
skin to legitimize sin." Like these pastors, others must stand up with faith
and influence the godly remnant in order to restore the moral
fabric of our nation.

You cannot be like the hypocrites and talk about principles
and live by preferences. Inconsistency will dilute and destroy

> You cannot be like the hypocrites and talk about principles and live by preferences. Inconsistency will dilute and destroy your godly influence.

your godly influence. For example, sometimes we wonder why we lose our adult children to the world, since they have grown up in the Church. Many times it is because of their parents' or some other authority figure's hypocrisy. They saw adults raise their hands in church but could not reconcile that image with flamboyant homosexuals in the choir loft, pornography under their parents' mattress and a pastor who compromised by winking at sin instead of confronting it. In other words, they were disillusioned by adults who talked about principles but lived by preferences. You must realize that such inconsistency will destroy your testimony and influence.

It is one thing to say, "Well, yes, I have convictions." Do you hold them so strongly that you are truly committed to them? Do you live by them no matter what? Someone reading this may say, "Well, I don't know that I believe anything so much that there would not be a reason that I would give it up. Everything is relative." Well, let me ask you a few questions.

- Do you believe that Jesus Christ is the Son of God and the judge of all men (see Hebrews 12:23; 1 John 5:5)?
- Do you believe that only the pure in heart will see God and that we must be holy in all we do (see Matthew 5:8; 1 Peter 1:15–16)?
- Do you believe that one day you will stand before God and give an account of your life (see Romans 14:9–12)?
- Do you believe that Jesus is the way, the truth and the life and that no one has access to the Father or eternal life in heaven except through Him (see John 14:6)?
- Do you believe that the promise of your own resurrection rests in Christ's resurrection (see Romans 6:5)?
- Do you believe that one day Jesus is coming back to receive unto Himself those who are ready (see Matthew 24:30–44)?
- Are these basic convictions in your life?

Someone might say, "Well, some of that I believe, and some I don't." You know what, that person might be a good candidate to be a "celebrity" for the counterfeit influence—by saying whatever Satan and other people want to hear. Anyone who is double-minded in his or her Christian beliefs will not be a godly influence (see James 1:6–8). Beloved, you cannot waver. As believers, we are called not to be conformed to the world but rather to be transformed by the renewing of our minds.

The Message translates Paul saying it this way in Romans 12:2: "Don't become so well-adjusted to your culture that you fit into it without even thinking. Instead, fix your attention on God. You'll be changed from the inside out." And people with renewed minds change their culture when they have renewed conviction. This is important. In order to be a godly influence, you must be totally sold out to God. If you are not committed to your convictions, you will move from conviction to compromise, from principle to preference, from "folk" to "yolk," from civil rights to gay rights (and whatever rhyme and reasoning is socially acceptable).

The Church seemingly has a defeatist attitude when it comes to confronting giant social issues and ideologies. We have lost influence in the world regarding these issues, many times because of our responses. Religious extremists have judged people, instead of sin, with a "burn in hell" attitude void of God's love. They have forgotten that faith expresses itself through love (see Galatians 5:6) and that human anger does not produce the righteousness that God desires (see James 1:20). On the other hand, "sloppy agape" Christians have acquiesced and compromised with a watered-down, cross-less Gospel for the sake of more money and members. They have forgotten that friendship with the world's system is hatred toward God (see James 4:4); they have forsaken their first love and tolerate sin (see Revelation 2:4, 20). There is a remnant, however, that is fighting Satan, the real enemy. And God will use their faith-filled prayers, love and action to set a nation free.

Remember the secret of the "folk" and "yolk" example and what we have learned from David and Nehemiah. It takes only one person saying the truth, even in the midst of mass error, to break the power of falsehood. Bear in mind that if we waver, we will not have any influence with others. But if we cry out with conviction and persistence, godly influence will prevail. We may have to repeat it a few times, perhaps even for a lifetime, but eventually the light of truth will dispel the darkness of deception. People will begin to say, "That was illogical. What was I saying? Why did I believe that in the first place?"

All God wants you to do, even when a nation is in error, is to have conviction, speak the truth in love and fight in intercession. Your faith will invoke God into the battle, and He will fight for you. Remember, the depth of your convictions will determine the power of your influence. God will use your persistence to change the prevailing influence that reigns over others. We must pick up our stones of faith and war against the mindsets of the giants in our day with intercession and sacrifice. Like David and Nehemiah, instead of rehearsing the size of the task and our opposition, let's rehearse the history of God's faithfulness. Giant strongholds can tumble down through prayer and sacrifice, just as they have during other times in history.

God Can Do It Again!

No one thought slavery could be abolished after the Supreme Court's 1857 Dred Scott decision, which said slaves had no rights. In the Jim Crow era, people who grew up in the South thought racial strongholds would never be abolished and segregation would stay an accepted cultural norm. But because of prayer, revival and action, these prevailing strongholds were broken through godly influence. The influence shifted so radically that slavery and segregation became irrational. We even have museums reminding us of how bad these eras were so that we do not repeat these past mistakes. Once accepted norms, slavery and segregation are now considered absurdities in our society!

Recalling what we learned from our "folk" and "yolk" exercise, we must respond with loving conviction and cry out from the rooftops, "Egg white!" Somebody must shout, "God's hand can save and deliver people from homosexuality!" Someone must proclaim, "God can break the power of false ideologies and end abortion!" A generation must arise and declare, "God will help us rebuild the torn-down walls of our nation and send revival!" With God we can defeat the Goliaths of our day, and His truth can set a nation free. People full of love, faith and conviction must arise in this hour. And in our obedient stand, we must trust the results to God, regardless of the consequences.

We see this in the case of Shadrach, Meshach and Abednego. When they went into exile in Babylon, they gained favor with King Nebuchadnezzar (see Daniel 1:19). And then, after Daniel interpreted Nebuchadnezzar's dream, they had such incredible favor that they were promoted to some of the highest positions in Babylon (see Daniel 2:48–49). We know the familiar story, of course. The day came for everyone to bow down to Nebuchadnezzar's image of gold, but the three Hebrew boys took a stand and refused to do so, because they were people of conviction (see Daniel 3:12). Instead of being thrown into the fiery furnace immediately, however, because they had so much favor with the king, they were given a second chance. But even in secret, away from the crowd, they still refused to bow down (see Daniel 3:13–18). Public passion should always be the by-product of private devotion. The true test of character is who you are when no one can see you.

I love their response. Basically, they said, "King, we will not bow down to your god, and we believe that our God is able to deliver us from the fiery furnace. But even if He doesn't deliver us, we will not bow down to your god." What moves the heart of God is an "even if" person. "Even if He doesn't heal me today, He's still worthy; and He will heal me later. Even if I lose my job because I won't bend the rules, He's still worthy; and He will open doors for me another way."

We all know the ending of this story. The Lord stood in the midst of the fire with Shadrach, Meshach and Abednego. No harm came to them, because God is a very present help in times of trouble (see Psalm 46:1). The weapon of their enemies was formed, but it did not prosper (see Isaiah 54:17). Nebuchadnezzar knew how to intimidate and manipulate people, but these Hebrew boys knew how to move the heart of God. Hold your applause, however!

We often end the story right there. But it is important to note that Daniel's account goes on to say that Nebuchadnezzar made a new decree over the entire kingdom. The king decreed that no one in Babylon could say anything against the God of Shadrach, Meshach and Abednego (see Daniel 3:29). This happened because they influenced Nebuchadnezzar instead of Nebuchadnezzar influencing them. When you courageously put favor with man at risk, God will release His influence through you. From this we see what happens when just a few people stand with God. Their stand can result in God's influence being released and decrees over nations being changed. (Now, please feel free to shout!)

We see this in the book of Esther. In Esther 4:14, Mordecai said to Esther, "If you remain silent at this time, relief and deliverance for the Jews will arise from another place, but you and your father's family will perish. And who knows but that you have come to royal position for such a time as this?"

Please indulge me while I give you the unofficial Will Ford translation of this verse. I believe if you were to read between the lines, so to speak, what Mordecai was really saying was, "Esther, you're cute and all. And I know you won a beauty pageant. The new dresses you have look a whole lot better than the orphan rags you used to wear. God has truly favored you. I hate to burst your bubble, but the favor you have is not just about you. Your favor is related to a purpose. You can use your favor to serve yourself, or you can trade it for influence and save a nation. Esther, will you try to save only yourself, or will you try to save us all?" Favor that is selfishly used is abused and forfeits our opportunity to be a godly influence.

Esther rose to the occasion and broke the death decree over her generation, and so must we today.

The Cost of Discipleship

Releasing influence, as part of taking up one's cross, is costly. We see this, of course, in the life of our Lord and Savior, Jesus Christ. In the Old Testament, we see this in the lives of Moses, Daniel and Esther. In modern history, we see this in the life of William Wilberforce, who played a critical role in ending slavery in England. Wilberforce was threatened, mocked and jeered for forty years. Nevertheless, his godly influence prevailed and broke the back of slavery.

Later we see that God released heavenly influence through Martin Luther King Jr., breaking demonic decrees of segregation and racism. There is an old adage that says, "If a man hasn't found something he's willing to die for, he isn't fit to live," and Dr. King gave his life for what he believed. He put any favor he had as a nice middle-class preacher's son at risk and gave his life in order to influence history. In everyday life and work, we must stand in faith and be obedient to God and entrust the results and consequences to Him.

My favorite example of this today is Linda Rios Brook. The story of her journey can be read in Linda's book *Wake Me When It's Over: From the Boardroom to the Twilight Zone and the Faithfulness of God* (PublishAmerica, 2001).

Linda, who is a leader in cultural transformation through the workplace, once was a leader in the media. She was president and general manager of a television station in Minnesota, and the station's ratings were among the best in that region. A devout Christian, Linda led a Bible study in her church and also spoke at various community prayer breakfasts.

One day Linda was surprised to find herself on the cover of a local tabloid newspaper. The article questioned whether or not the chief executive of a major news organization would be impartial about news coverage if she were a Christian. Following company protocol, she informed her superiors of the article.

Shortly afterward, the media company that owned her station informed Linda that she was not allowed to speak publicly about her faith and must stop leading the Bible study in her church. Unable to comply, Linda resigned from her position.

God was so honored by Linda's obedience that He opened another door for her. A group of Christian businessmen approached her about starting a Christian television station in the same market. They bought a small station out of bankruptcy and hired her as president and general manager. Seven years later, through the sale of the property, Linda netted the shareholders a 1,600 percent return on their investments!

Because Linda is a person who lives by conviction and principles when there is a cost for doing so, God rewarded her obedience by releasing His influence through her. She traded favor with man for favor with God. Her faith had substance and financial benefits as well.

What Sanballat and Tobiah have gripped your thought life with intimidation? What fearful grip has held your family captive, preventing your loved ones from moving forward? What Goliath have you been called to pray and act against in your city? Motivated by love, stand in faith. Remember, the depth of your conviction will determine the power of your influence. Persist in prayer with conviction, and you will replace death with life by the fruit of God's Word of truth. In order to be a godly influence, you must be a person of substantive faith. If you are, you will be an anointed vessel of honor fit for the Master's use.

EXERCISING INFLUENCE *through Prayer*

Father, forgive me for allowing toxic influence in my life through music, television, books and other media. I also repent of lingering with people and environments detrimental to my faith. Forgive me for areas of sin and compromise in which I have lived by my preferences instead of Your principles. God, I value what You say, so please deepen my conviction for Your Word.

On behalf of the Church, I ask forgiveness for our haughtiness and hypocrisy and for the judgment seats we have erected, and I ask that You replace them with Your mercy seats. O Lord, cleanse us and release compassion and power through the Church to set the captives free. I thank You that the consequences of every sexual sin—from pornography and promiscuity to homosexuality and abortion—were mercifully paid for at the cross. In addition to saving their souls, heal and deliver people from sexual bondage and broken identities.

Thank You for the sanctity of marriage between man and woman. In Jesus' name, we resist demonic, same-sex legislation and its influence in every branch of government. Like Nehemiah and David, we recall the history of Your faithfulness, and we declare that the same God who ended slavery will end abortion also. We stand in the exposed places and speak life to this nation! In Jesus' name, Amen.

5

The Anointing
and the Fragrant Life

IT BOGGLES MY MIND that one human being can step into a forest bristling with activity and scatter every animal just by the scent of his or her flesh. Have you ever thought about that? The human scent carries such influence that every animal, great or small, within a certain radius will sniff to discern that human's next move in order to defend or flee its territory. Now, I know you are thinking, *Hey, I know that guy! I went to high school with him. His reputation for body odor was so bad, he could part a crowded hallway like the Red Sea. That's why we called him Moses! He didn't have an odor; he had an "oh, dear." He didn't have a scent; he had a smell. We didn't defend our territory, either; we just ran. So what's the big deal about stinky animal influence, and what's your point, Preacher?*

Okay, so maybe you were not thinking that—but I was. (Now I am the one with the bad reputation after that attempt at humor!)

But seriously, there is a spiritual significance regarding a scent (not a smell)—that is, a fragrant aroma that carries influence. Christ, our bright Morning Star, has an aromatic fragrance that carries influence set apart for those in relationship with Him. This fragrance is so powerful that it changes reputations; so there is hope for "Moses," and there is hope for me. And there is hope for you, too. I am talking about another manifestation of the Holy Spirit, like faith, that is a substance: the anointing. Another reason King David had influence was that he was chosen, anointed and set apart unto the Lord (see 1 Samuel 16:13).

In this chapter, you will understand spheres of influence and the ministry focus of the anointing. You will also see how the anointing builds our character and indirectly influences others. You were called to have a fragrant relationship with Christ, the Anointed One, and be set apart unto Him. The aroma of the anointing carries influence, similar to the effects of human scent upon the animal kingdom.

Adam, Is That You?

Hollywood loves to make surreal movies about animal dominion on planet earth. In reality, it could be that the only thing that keeps your downtown from looking like a scene from *Planet of the Apes* is the chemical makeup of the scent of human beings, which evokes respect from animals. Creation scientists and theologians say that when humans show up in a forest, the animals still do a double take because the remembrance of Adam's scent is in their DNA. Before the Fall, the scent of man was an aroma of life, and they were attracted to humans. But now, due to our fallen nature, a whiff of unfamiliar human flesh is an aroma of death to animals, causing them to run for their lives.

104

On the other hand, animals will also associate the scent of a human with loving treatment. Their fear is turned to respect when they discover that the one they should fear the most is the one who loves them the most. When our distinct human scent is associated with help rather than harm, then our scent conveys good influence. This explains why animals mightier than us, like horses and elephants, feel compelled to submit their strength and power to the authority and influence of puny human trainers or a ringmaster in a circus. Seems like these big animals should say, "Hey, the wrong one is giving the orders here!" (or as my kids say, "You ain't the boss of me!") and elephants should make humans jump through hoops held by monkeys, or at least threaten to do so, but that is not the case.

As a matter of fact, seasoned animal trainers are rarely hurt by animals, because they know how to wield their authority. Animals inherently know that they do not have the right to rule over humans. Otherwise we could get run out of town by an organized coup attempt even of smaller creatures, as in Alfred Hitchcock's movie *The Birds*. Animals have power but not authority and influence over us. Rather, we have influence—just with a whiff of our scent—over them.

In the spirit realm, the fragrance of the anointing carries influence. In 2 Corinthians 2:14–16 (which will be discussed in greater length later), Paul says that we are God's fragrance of life to some and an aroma of death to others. This explains why some people are attracted to the anointing we have while others are repelled by it because they are in bondage to the kingdom of darkness. This also explains what happens in the invisible realm.

Similar to the effect a human being has upon the animals when entering a forest, when an anointed person approaches, the spirit beings within the radius or sphere of influence of that person come to attention. They wait to discern the person's next move. I imagine an angel smelling the aroma of our anointing and saying to another angel, "Who is that man, that God is mindful of him?" or "I can't wait to see how God has us minister in response to this little woman's prayers." They draw near, because the anointing is an aroma of life to them. But when demons catch a whiff of the anointing, I imagine them saying, "How do we protect this turf?" or "Let's plan our exit strategy—are there any pigs around?" (see Mark 5:12). They are repelled, because the anointing is an aroma of death to them.

Angels and demons do a double take when you are anointed, because you have the fragrance of the last Adam, Jesus Christ! *Christ* means "anointed one," and when a Christian, or "little anointed one," shows up, it evokes awe, fear and respect from the kingdom of darkness. Just as animals more powerful than humans inherently know they do not have the right to rule over humans, the devil, though powerful, knows he does not have the right or authority to rule over Christians. Neither does he have the right to use his supernatural strength on us. We see this in two key biblical terms.

Dunamis and Exousia

Please pay close attention while I briefly get a little detailed in explaining this. It will be helpful. There are two key Greek words relevant to our discussion that are translated "power" in the New Testament. One word is *dunamis*, which means "supernatural ability, miraculous force or power." The other word is *exousia*, used by Paul in Colossians 1:13, where he says that God "hath delivered us from the power [*exousia*] of darkness, and hath translated us into the kingdom of his dear Son" (KJV). *Exousia*, according to *Strong's Concordance*, means not only "superhuman power" but also "authority, right, jurisdiction, magistrate"—and my favorite, "delegated influence"!

What Colossians 1:13 is saying is that in Christ we have been delivered from the right of the enemy to use his power on us, because we are no longer under the enemy's jurisdiction and delegated influence! Paul goes on to say that we have been "translated" or taken out of the enemy's kingdom and placed under the jurisdiction of a Kingdom superior to the powers of darkness! In other words, "He ain't the boss of me!"—or you, either, if you are a Christian.

But wait, it gets better. In Luke 10:19, Jesus used these two words for power: "I have given you authority to trample on snakes and scorpions and to overcome all the power of the enemy; nothing will harm you." The Greek word for "authority" here is *exousia*, and the word translated "power" is *dunamis*. Inserting these words and definitions, this verse reads as follows: "I have given you *exousia* [superhuman power, authority, right and delegated influence] to trample on snakes and scorpions and to overcome all the *dunamis* [supernatural force and miraculous power] of the enemy; nothing will harm you."

Jesus was saying that our right and delegated influence, in Him, controls the enemy's supernatural power! Since we are children of God, the evil one has no legal right to harm us (see 1 John 5:18–19). Like an animal trainer who knows how to use his or her authority with creatures greater in strength, those who are anointed for an assignment will not be harmed by anything when they know how to wield their authority and use their influence in the spiritual realm.

If you are a Christian and you have been jumping through hoops of depression and negative thoughts and behaviors, maybe it is time you realize you do not have to take orders from an evil ringmaster. To say it bluntly, the wrong one is giving the orders! The devil has had you in his circus long enough. You do not have to submit to him any longer; rather, he must submit to the delegated influence you have in Jesus' name. It is time to get out of the devil's sideshow and shut it down. It is time to tell the devil when to leave and where to go, in Jesus' name.

As you can see, there is a difference between having force or power and the right or authority to use it. In *Intercessory Prayer* (Regal, 1996), Dutch Sheets writes, "Power does the work, but authority controls the power." He also says:

> Satan still has all the inherent powers and abilities he has always had. He "prowls about like a roaring lion" (1 Peter 5:8). And, contrary to what some teach, he still has his teeth. He still has "fiery darts" (Ephesians 6:16 KJV). If you don't believe this, try going without your armor. What he lost was the right (authority) to use his power on those who make Jesus Lord. However, Satan is a thief and a lawbreaker and will use his power or abilities on us anyway if we don't understand that through Christ we now have authority over him and his power. *Authority is the issue.*

Now don't get carried away and run out and start the First Church of Exousia! Some have tried that. Understand that all of this is exercised through the realm of authority for which God has anointed us. No anointing for the task yields no fragrance for the moment, resulting in no influence or power. Therefore, the important questions are "What task or assignment has God anointed me for and delegated to me?" and "What is my sphere of influence?" Just as you do not want to go without your spiritual armor because you know the enemy has power, you do not want to pick an arbitrary fight with the devil just because you have authority. Doing either one is spiritually ignorant—and could be painful. If you do not believe me, move beyond your assigned jurisdiction and go poke your neighbor's pit bull in the nose and tell it to sit. You will get bitten!

> When authority is abused, influence is lost. Authority, power and influence are to be wielded, stewarded and respected.

You can also get hurt spiritually, so do not operate in pride or presumption. When authority is abused, influence is lost. Authority, power and influence are to be wielded, stewarded and respected. This is why Jesus said we are to rejoice not that demons are compelled to submit to us in His name but rather that our names are written in heaven (see Luke 10:20).

You must know, therefore, what God has delegated to you, the purpose for your influence and the reason for your anointing. Is it for a task? For a calling? For a region? For a season? These factors determine your sphere of influence. You cannot know this without spending intimate time with God, which is the primary purpose of the anointing. That being said, let's get a better grasp on the purpose of the anointing. The first aspect is that the anointing represents a heart consecrated and set apart for intimacy with God.

Set Apart and Spiritually Attractive

People get excited when they talk about the anointing. That is because the anointing grants you, as God's representative, favor. Your words, gifts and talents carry power when you have been saturated by His supernatural presence. It is like going from a hand saw to a power saw in ministry. But the lesson we learn from the first anointed priesthood, Aaron and his sons, is that the primary focus of the anointing was to minister unto the Lord (see Exodus 30:30). The anointing prepared the priests for direct intimacy with God, and the people indirectly benefited from the atmosphere created by the priests' fragrant relationship with Him.

Of course, ministry unto the Lord will lead you to touch people's lives and minister to others. And God will give you His heart for them so that as you minister, you represent His heart. But the focus is still on God, as a service requested by

hich brings pleasure to God (see John 5:30; see also
~~~~ ~~.10). If we base ministry only on meeting the needs and
desires of people, we run the risk of doing the will of people
and misrepresenting the will of God.

The high priest Aaron abused his anointing and gifting as an
artisan to please the idolatrous desire of the people by making
a golden calf for them to worship (see Exodus 32:1–6). Yielding
to their pressure, Aaron misrepresented God and led the nation
back into idolatry instead of away from it, and many people
died as a result (see Exodus 32:35). Simply put, if you please
God, you will serve people, but if you please people, sooner or
later you will stop serving God's will to the detriment of others. You must understand that you are separated to the Lord
for His purposes, because people are drawn to you when you
are anointed.

The anointing is a fragrant perfume, and perfume in the Bible
represents either seduction (see Proverbs 7:17) or influence (see
Proverbs 27:9; Song of Songs 1:3). Like a perfume fragrance,
anointed people are attractive, spiritually speaking. You can be
either an anointed influencer who is a "star," introducing others to God, or a seductively perfumed "celebrity" who draws
people to yourself. This is why we must be dead to popularity,
fame and praise.

Anointing and Death to Self

An aspect of the anointing that we do not like to discuss is that
it also prepared people for death (see Mark 14:8; 16:1). Now,
the good news is that the Bible reveals that death is beyond
physical finality. Everyone will spend eternity in either heaven
or hell. Christians will be eternally separated from Satan, and
unbelievers will be eternally separated from God. Death, therefore, means a separation of relationship. Just as physical death

is emotionally painful because of the separation of relationship, so is spiritual death as God removes the rivals from our hearts. The Lord is a jealous God; therefore, we are to be dead or separated from sin, self, negative relationships and people's opinions.

You see, the Lord wants to use anointed people who are dead to selfish ambition, dead to popularity and dead to the praise of men. There is nothing wrong with being affirmed or honored; we all need that to a degree. But what I am confronting is craving the validation of others. The validation of your calling is not the applause of people. Neither is it your ministry results; that is God's glory, and He does not share that spotlight. The anointing alone is God's approval and validation of you—period (see Joshua 13:14, 33).

In other words, God's presence *is* our reward. Sometimes He will lead us to rest in His peace and sometimes He will lead us to do great works through His power—but the reward is the same. The outcomes of God's presence and power are wonderful, but the bottom line is that He is our reward. Focusing on ministry results for validation will turn us into Christian Houdinis: We will always be trying to top the last trick, revelation or miracle so we can keep people coming to our performance or show, supposedly in Jesus' name.

This is what happens when ministry results are measured by multitudes of people rather than by the loving magnitude of Christ's finished work on the cross. When you have the approval and acceptance of Christ, the most powerful Person in heaven and earth, who cares about worldly validation? This is important because when you are anointed, as God's representative, you will say things others do not want to hear. You cannot let man's acceptance or crowd-pleasing, therefore, be an influence in your life.

We must allow the anointing to address the self-life. We must die to self so that we are not swayed by worldly influence. As

Jesus was anointed by Mary for His death on the cross (see John 12:3–7), we also are anointed for death to self in order that we may go to a deeper place of intimacy with Him. We can share in the cry of Paul's heart: "I want to know Christ and the power of his resurrection and the fellowship of sharing in his sufferings, becoming like him in his death, and so, somehow, to attain to the resurrection from the dead" (Philippians 3:10–11).

There is no resurrection without a death. Though the anointing is released outwardly as a fragrance, it must be worked inwardly as a medicinal ointment to purify our heart motives. The anointing ministers to your heart like a balm as you go through difficult times in your life (see Jeremiah 8:22; 51:8). We shortchange ourselves when we do not allow the crucible of life's circumstances and the Holy Spirit to shape our character. It seems that everyone in the Church today wants resurrection power, but most do not want to die to self (see 1 Corinthians 15:31). Beloved, Jesus was anointed for a cross, and so are we. One of the greatest aspects of taking up our cross is forgiving others.

Forgiveness and Influence

When you are anointed, you will practice forgiving others. What do I mean? Do not be surprised when others around you are provoked to jealousy and envy because of your anointing. Once you stop playing the world's system and die to self, you will begin to manifest Christ's resurrection power in varying degrees. Over time the intimacy and power you have from God will expose the deficient power, lack of substance, shallowness and hypocrisy in others. Thus the enemy tries to block your anointing and influence by attacking you through spiteful people under his control. You must remember, however, that dead people do not flinch. This is all part of the enemy's strategy to get you to embrace a victim mentality. You have been called to be a victor who is dead to attacks on your reputation and to being mistreated.

King David undoubtedly had influence because he did not allow unforgiveness, which is one of Satan's greatest ploys to thwart our anointing and influence in prayer, to trap him. One of the reasons David had a fragrant prayer life is that he stayed free from bitterness. David had influence in prayer because he forgave Saul and Absalom. Do you want to know the greatest hindrance to the anointing being released in your life? It is not Satan or jealous people. It is this: your inability to forgive. Bitter hearts attract demonic torment, and Satan knows that your unforgiveness will block the spiritual influence of your prayer life (see Matthew 6:15; 18:35). It is the fly in our anointing or perfume (see Ecclesiastes 10:1) that taints our influence in prayer.

The greater the influence you have as God's representative, the smaller the margin of error, because many people's lives are affected by the impact of your own life. As Ecclesiastes 10:1 says, "As dead flies give perfume a bad smell, so a little folly outweighs wisdom and honor." A childhood memory helped me understand this Scripture.

Long ago, while visiting our grandparents, my cousins and I were playing with a perfume bottle our grandmother had thrown into the trash. It was a fancy French container with a sequined bulb atomizer that, when squeezed, sprayed the bottle's perfume. Well, we found that instead of being empty, the bottle still had lots of perfume in it. Curious about the type of perfume and why this pretty bottle was in the trash, we squeezed the spray bulb to see if it worked. Instead of releasing a sweet smell, it filled the air with a nasty odor. Fortunately, no one was sprayed directly. The smell was so horrible we had to leave the room and quarantine it! We learned later that our grandmother had thrown away this bottle because a fly had flown into it. She knew a dead fly makes perfume smell bad, and boy, did it! This smell was so bad that even today nobody has accepted the blame for squeezing the bulb.

Similarly, this proverb is about the anointing (perfume), you the vessel (bottles) and demonic activity and sin (flies). When we succumb to temptation, sinful folly will corrupt us, thus destroying our influence and reputation. As God's vessels of honor, we can taint our influence by tolerating sin, and we can eventually destroy our influence by participating in sin. If we do not guard our hearts, instead of being a fragrant aroma we can become a stench in God's nostrils (see Isaiah 65:5). When you think of formerly honorable ministers, politicians, entertainers or athletes, how many times must you fan away their fumes? Whatever they do or endorse does not come to mind; instead, the first thing you think about is some foul sex scandal or other stinking malady. Regrettably, their godly influence has been diminished by sin. And like the stench in my grandmother's house, no one wants to be involved with them, no matter how fancy they look in the pulpit, on the entertainment stage or in the political arena. Yes, God is a restorer, but sometimes it takes a while for sinful memories to be fumigated.

David had to go through his own fumigation process because of his failure with Bathsheba. Yet because he allowed God to work on his heart, his relationship with God—and years later his reputation—was restored. We must allow the anointing to work in us and allow God to exfoliate character flaws in our hearts so that we die to fleshly motives. As a result, when the flies of demonic temptation come, they will not find a filthy place to land in our hearts.

Anointing and Transfer

Another aspect of the anointing is that it is transferable. Through His authority, Christ makes us delegated distributors of His power. I want to share with you a powerful example of this. At a conference in Washington, D.C., I felt prompted by the Holy Spirit to impart to an individual I met there an anointing for dreams. This is a sphere of gifting that God has granted to me and sometimes has me activate in others through prayer. I assumed this young man must be a dreamer, but he told me that, up to that point, he was not aware of his dreams. I prayed for him nonetheless, going off the unction I had, to receive Holy Spirit-inspired dreams. I was not sure what happened, but I saw him one year later, and he told me an amazing story.

After that prayer, my friend left for a ministry trip—and had his first significant dream. In the dream he entered a retail store and saw someone who had a cast on his leg. He knew that God wanted to do something, so asked if he could pray for healing. After prayer, the individual began walking around the store and soon was completely healed. Sensing that the dream was significant my friend wrote it down, noting the feeling that was still residing in his heart.

Three days later, my friend entered a hardware store, and saw a boy with his arm in a sling. After a moment, he realized that the sense he had in his spirit was very similar to what he had felt in the dream. He introduced himself to this fourteen-year-old and learned that he had broken his collar bone just three days before. The doctors were going to have to do surgery and insert a metal plate to align the bones.

My friend asked if he could pray for him, and, after having done so, asked if the pain was better. The boy replied that it was "90 percent better!" So he continued praying, asking for full restoration of the arm. After this last prayer, the boy looked at him, thanked him and walked away. Meanwhile, he went on with his shopping.

About five minutes later, the fourteen-year-old ran up to my friend with his dad. He was ecstatic. He said, "I don't know what you did, but my arm feels great!" He started moving his arm, which he could not do before.

My friend said, "Jesus healed you, and through this He is revealing Himself to you. He wants to have a relationship with you." The young man then prayed with my friend to receive Christ—right in the store, with his father sobbing next to him. It turns out that his father was praying for him to give his life to the Lord!

Later the boy emailed my friend to confirm that he was healed, and the doctors would not need to do surgery!

God definitely did not need my prayer for my friend back at the conference in Washington, D.C., nor did He need prayers for the young man—but He *chose* to need us, which is humbling, is it not? Now the fragrant knowledge of Christ's victory is spreading wherever this story goes.

Friends of the Bridegroom

In Bible days, kings had elaborate parades or processions full of pomp and grandeur. There were two types of celebration processions: one for victory over an embattled region and another for weddings. In both of these processions, incense, perfume and fragrances were burned and released, representing the presence of the king, the atmosphere of his kingdom and his increasing influence. An example of this is the bridal procession of King Solomon in Song of Songs 3:6–8:

> Who is this coming up from the desert like a column of smoke, perfumed with myrrh and incense made from all the spices of the merchant? Look! It is Solomon's carriage, escorted by sixty warriors, the noblest of Israel, all of them wearing the sword, all experienced in battle, each with his sword at his side, prepared for the terrors of the night.

The sixty warriors accompanying King Solomon's wedding procession were friends of the groom, which was common. But these friends were also the noblest and most experienced soldiers in Israel, probably Solomon's royal bodyguard. He was coming with his expensive dowry, which was given to the parents to compensate for the loss of income as a result of the daughter's departure. The money and possessions in this dowry were very valuable, which explains why these warriors were necessary to protect against thieves. The king was also taking no chances in safeguarding his bride. Yes, these warriors were celebrating the king's wedding, but they were also advancing in this procession, willing to war against everything that hindered the king, his bride and their love for each other. And as they went forward, they released a fragrant aroma into the atmosphere.

The other celebration procession that used perfume was the victory parade of kings and generals, as alluded to by Paul in 2 Corinthians 2:14–16 (NASB):

> But thanks be to God, who always leads us in triumph in Christ, and manifests through us the sweet aroma of the knowledge of Him in every place. For we are a fragrance of Christ to God among those who are being saved and among those who are perishing; to the one an aroma from death to death, to the other an aroma from life to life. And who is adequate for these things?

Warren Wiersbe, in *Wiersbe's Expository Outlines on the New Testament* (Victor, 1992), writes the following in regard to this passage:

> The picture in vv. 14–17 was familiar to every Roman but not to 20th century Christians. Whenever a victorious general returned home from battle, Rome gave him a public parade, not unlike our modern ticker tape parades. This parade was filled with pomp and glory, and a great deal of incense was burned

in honor of the hero. In the parade soldiers and officers would enjoy glory and praise, but slaves and captives also present would end up in the arena to die fighting the wild beasts. As the victors smelled the incense, they inhaled an aroma of life and joy; but to the captives, the incense was a reminder of their coming death.

Of these two celebration processions mentioned in Scripture, one celebrated a conquered territory, while the other celebrated a conquering love. We need to understand both of these processions to appreciate fully our relationship with our victorious Bridegroom King, Jesus Christ.

On the cross, He conquered every foe. His precious blood is the dowry used to purchase His Bride, the Church. The columns of smoke from incense and perfume represent His presence, the atmosphere of His Kingdom and His expanding influence. The incense also represents the prayers and praise of God's anointed saints (see Revelation 5:8). We ride in this procession with Him, sharing His victory while releasing our fragrant worship. As friends of the Bridegroom, we are also wielding "the sword of the Spirit, which is the word of God" (Ephesians 6:17)—engaging the enemy in battle, because the Kingdom of God is advanced by forceful believers (see Matthew 11:12).

We press on in His parade of history, influenced by the atmosphere of His dominion, increasing the knowledge of His victory for His bride, the Church. When the aroma of His Kingdom is present, those who want the new life of that Kingdom rejoice, while those who are part of Satan's kingdom discern that this is an aroma of death and plan their exit strategy or battle to hold lost territory. Though defeated, the demonic kingdom also tries to rob others of freedom and attempts to stop the increasing knowledge of Christ's victory. The demonic powers can smell change in the atmosphere and realize that their dominion is over, so they try to resist the new government, the Kingdom of God. As anointed friends of the Bridegroom, we thus war against every thought and argument that hinders the Kingdom of truth (see 2 Corinthians 10:3–5).

So we see that Jesus' bridal procession is a warring victory parade that is ever increasing the influence and knowledge of His Kingdom's dominion over Satan.

Aroma of Death v. Aroma of Life

One example of Christ's victorious procession and dominion over the enemy's death procession is found in Luke 7:11–17. This story is an awesome illustration of the warring bridal procession celebrating the victory of our King over the kingdom of darkness and of our King's ever-increasing influence.

According to Jewish custom, when a procession came through the streets, everyone had to stop out of reverence and allow the procession to pass by. We see this practiced today in American towns and cities as traffic respectfully stops for police-escorted funeral processions. But we have a dilemma in this story. There are two processions: a funeral procession and a victory parade celebrating our Bridegroom King Jesus, who has a growing reputation for His healing ministry and now has a large crowd joyfully following Him.

At the gate of the town of Nain, Jesus' parade was intersected by a great procession of gloom—people mourning the untimely death of a widow's only son, a young man still in his prime, robbed of life by the enemy. In the natural realm, the Lord's atmosphere of joy clashed with the funeral customs of the day: sad music, tearful mourners dressed in black and professional wailers in the streets. There is even more happening in the spiritual realm, however. What we have here is Satan's procession of death, claiming the dominion of his kingdom as the prevailing influence in the city of Nain, which means "beautiful."

CREATED FOR INFLUENCE ·

Satan seems to be glorifying death, parading his dominion of darkness in the streets and basically saying to the Lord, "You must yield to me; I'm the prevailing influence in the city of Nain. Isn't death beautiful?" By Jewish custom, if two processions met together at intersections or city gates, everyone had to yield to the funeral procession and allow it to pass first. But Jesus seems to be saying by His actions, "No, devil, I don't yield to you; you must yield to *My* Kingdom. I am here to restore Nain's beauty"—and He advances first through the gate in order to heal the young man.

You may be asking, Was Jesus out of order? The answer, of course, is no. But why? In Israel, the only procession that superseded or took priority over a funeral procession was a bridal procession. Jesus, our Bridegroom King, advanced His procession by raising this young man from the dead! A funeral procession was transformed into a victory parade celebrating the triumph of our Bridegroom King over death.

Is it not awesome that *Christ* means "anointed one"? Here we see the effects of the Anointed One's fragrant presence. No longer under the evil dominion of the stench of death, this young man is now under the influence of the fragrant aroma of life in Christ's Kingdom. Those in the funeral procession who had been weeping are now rejoicing and praising God. The knowledge of this victory was reported, and Jesus' influence increased: "'A great prophet has appeared among us,' they said. 'God has come to help his people.' This news about Jesus spread throughout Judea and the surrounding country" (Luke 7:16–17).

Death was overcome by life. Not only did the Lord refuse to yield to the enemy, but He totally changed the devil's agenda by turning a funeral procession into a parade celebrating His Kingdom life. When we are under the fragrant aroma and influence of Christ's Kingdom, everything changes: the atmosphere, circumstances and people's lives and hearts.

The gates of a city, which is where this miracle occurred, were places of influence administered by kings and judges to release justice in different matters. Here we see that King Jesus exercised His *exousia* as a magistrate and released justice in this matter by raising this young man from the dead. He restored Nain's beauty by replacing the mourners' ashes with a crown of beauty (see Isaiah 61:3). Christ's influence increased, and the gates of hell could not prevail against His dominion (see Matthew 16:18).

> You are the fragrant aroma that God uses in His procession to change the atmosphere. What a privilege!

There is a key element that we must understand about this Kingdom reality. According to 2 Corinthians 2:14, as a Christian, or "little anointed one," you are the fragrant aroma that God uses in His procession to change the atmosphere. What a privilege! As Kingdom citizens, we are anointed kings and priests who manifest a fragrant aroma, through our prayers and worship, wherever we go. As an anointed vessel of life, you are attracting people to the Kingdom, and as you advance God's Kingdom, your fragrant aroma is a reminder to demons of their doom. When an anointed person shows up, change is in the atmosphere.

While this is a beautiful picture, it is also a challenging reality. We have a tremendous responsibility as Christians. The enemy has paraded death around long enough in our streets. But with Christ's help, we can—through intercession—change death to life in the gates of our cities.

Restoring Manchester's Beauty

Perhaps you recall news clips about this happening in Manchester, Kentucky, several years ago. This area of Kentucky was known for drug addicts, crime and degradation. The drug problem was reportedly so bad that it had become an accepted part of the local economy, and the younger generation was literally dying off.

The condition looked hopeless. But all that changed when some friends of the Bridegroom decided to have a procession through town. Local pastors from various denominations held a prayer rally in the form of a march. In this prayer walk, they were declaring Christ's victory over the powers of darkness. They released a fragrant aroma through their intercession that changed the atmosphere of Manchester. They declared their city as Christ's territory and held up banners proclaiming His rule there.

The newspapers even picked up on this, with headlines like "Drug Dealers: Get Saved or Get Busted!" One prayer leader explained that the message of the march was clear: Drug users and dealers were doing wrong and needed to stop; thus, the marchers were praying for them to "get saved or get busted."

This marching procession of close to 3,500 people was a warring victory parade that was an aroma of life to those who desired Christ's freedom and an aroma of death to the demonic kingdom. Most felt that it was the forgiveness, repentance and unity of the pastors that brought the breakthrough in prayer. The fragrance of change was in the atmosphere.

In a region once known as the prescription painkiller capital of the nation, a prophetic march changed the prevailing influence of death and drugs. Even one of the most feared drug dealers in all of eastern Kentucky changed his life and accepted Christ. That's what I call being under the right influence!

One young lady was literally at death's door one night because of drugs, hiding in a closet and thinking she was about to die from an overdose. She cried out to God for help and experienced a visitation from the Lord that changed her life. Instead of the closet being this young woman's coffin, Christ broke the

enemy's hold—just as He did at Nain—and gave her new li.
Because of prayer, Jesus released justice on her behalf and did
what rehab did not do: He set her free!

Many have testified to change in the atmosphere of this community since the march of prayer and commitment. The beauty
of this "Nain" is being restored, and the prevailing influence
over the region has affected individuals and families and even
government. (For more about this story see http://www.cbn.
com/tv/1420536202001.)

God is giving intercessors an awesome privilege. It is the ability to carry out divine assignments revealed to them in the prayer
closet that will result in enormous influence upon the masses.
This is the hour in which intercession and action through divine
assignments will merge. For those who will not sell out to the
world but will sell out to God, extraordinary influence will be
released through them to advance His Kingdom.

Exercising Influence *through Prayer*

*Father, thank You for anointing me into intimacy with
You. Reveal to me the purpose for my anointing and grant
me uncanny favor so that I may be a godly influence for
You. I thank You for the delegated spheres of influence
I have personally, relationally, vocationally and territori-
ally. I thank You for new assignments to be an influence
for Your Kingdom.*

*I pray that You raise up a fragrant bridal army that will
change the atmosphere over regions, cities and nations.
Like Nain, our inner cities, suburbs and towns are longing
to be transformed into something beautiful.*

Lord, You hear the sound of Satan's dirge of death coming from gangster rap, hip hop, rock, death metal, goth and other music. Bridegroom King, pass through our gates, and interrupt Satan's procession of death again. Visit a subculture dressed in black for a funeral, and give them beauty for ashes. God, they are even singing, "Wake me up inside." Answer their cry, O Lord. Release a dream anointing that will resurrect their hopes again. Convict our children, draw them by Your Spirit and break the influence Satan has on them with his music. Raise up a generation that will worship You in spirit and in truth.

Bridegroom King, look at the devastation of drugs on our culture. Lay Your hands on every coffin of despair disguised as a crack house or crystal meth lab in our nation. We command the devil to release our sons and daughters! In the name of Jesus, we proclaim, "Drug dealers, get saved or get busted!" God, Your arm is not too short that it cannot reach. Turn and save them and use them for Your Kingdom. We thank You that angels are falling like leaves coming to our aid and demons are planning their exit strategies. In Jesus' name, Amen.

6

Kingdom Influence
in the Marketplace

GROWING UP, I REMEMBER my father telling me the story of a man who once went to Nelson Rockefeller to make him a business offer. Rockefeller decided not to do the deal, but as a consolation, he offered to allow the gentleman the opportunity of walking with him on the floor of the New York Stock Exchange. When Rockefeller walked on the floor of the exchange, everyone took notice of the person walking with him. Rockefeller lent the credibility of his trustworthy and powerful name to this man, and as a result, people who would not listen to him before were suddenly willing to hear what he had to offer. His words now had substance just because people knew him as the friend of Nelson Rockefeller. Rockefeller added importance and weight to this man. He was able to find investors for a multi-million-dollar deal simply because he walked with the right person.

Proverbs 22:1 says, "A good name is more desirable than great riches," for this very reason, because a credible reputation carries weight. This explains another definition of influence and helps us understand the next influential substance we will discuss: God's glory.

David was a person of godly influence because he pursued God's glory—not His praise but His substance and presence. David knew that Israel could not exist without God's glory, and David retrieved the Ark of the Covenant, which contained His glory. God's glory represents His presence and importance in our lives. It also represents our importance to Him, as He bestows His weight and influence upon us.

So in this chapter, we will talk about the influence of God's glory. We will look at how it empowers our authority and how it bestows God's importance to us. When you have God's glory, you can advance the Kingdom of heaven wherever He sends you. To get a better understanding, let's put on some "weight."

The Weight of God's Glory

Another dictionary definition of *influence* is "weight," in the sense of someone who conveys importance just by his or her presence. As in our Rockefeller example, when someone influential walks into a room, people know it. Whether his or her influence comes from the kingdom of darkness or from the Kingdom of light, people sense something when he or she walks into the room. Because of the substance he or she carries, the atmosphere changes when he or she walks into any environment or situation. People will even look around and say, "Who just walked into the room?"

The primary Hebrew word for glory in the Old Testament is *kabod*, which means "weighty presence." When Solomon dedicated the Temple, we see that the glory of God fell and the priests could not stand in order to minister (see 2 Chronicles 5:14). The atmosphere changed as God stepped into the room: The priests fell to the ground, coming under the weight of God's presence. And the Levites, who surely were impacted by God's glory also, rose up and carried the glory into society—as gate-keepers, worship minstrels, officials and judges (see 1 Chronicles 23:1–5). The priests and Levites had previously been anointed for service, but now—with God's glory upon them—they went to another level of influence.

Kabod was carried by those who had weight or importance. As they made decisions for their culture, their decisive words had weight because of their fellowship with God. The weight of His glory empowered their authority, and God released His influence through them to advance His Kingdom. With His glory, God bestowed upon them His importance.

What is wonderful is that, as we see in the book of Acts, we are to be partakers to a degree of the same glory. According to Acts 1 and 2, 120 disciples spent ten days in obedient fellow-ship with God in prayer. Much like their 120 forerunners in 2 Chronicles 5:12–14—the priests who were sounding trumpets when the glory fell at the dedication of the Temple—when the glory of God fell in the Upper Room, these "priests" had a hard time standing up as well.

As promised, on that particular Pentecost, God released an outpouring of epic proportions. And as a result of their intimate fellowship with Christ, when they used Jesus' name, He backed them up. You see, it is one thing to walk with a Rockefeller, but it is another thing altogether to walk with the Rock of Ages.

In the world, influence emanates from a force. But in the Kingdom of God, influence emanates from a Person. Not only could everyone recognize that these believers had been with Jesus by their words, they also saw that He still walked with them through the person of the Holy Spirit. Jesus' followers had the influence of heaven because He gave them the credibility of His name. This was possible because they had an intimate relationship with Christ. In other words, they were walking with the right Person.

For years, I struggled with the thought, *Am I full-time business, or full-time ministry?* Finally, I realized, "I'm full-time Kingdom!" You see, it is not about vocation; it is about God's call and assignment for our lives. Regardless of that place of work, we are to release the principles, morals, ethics, virtues and values of the Kingdom of heaven—in our homes, and in our jobs in the marketplace. When you are led by walking with the right Person, the vocation or place He takes you does not matter.

As Christ's followers walked into the room, so to speak, the whole atmosphere changed. People recognized their importance to God as He worked with the believers, performing signs, miracles and wonders. Lost people understood their importance to the Lord through the disciples' message of Christ's love for them. The weight of His glory produced incredible results. They spoke and ministered in great power and authority, and people received what they had to say. On the Day of Pentecost, about three thousand souls were added to the church (see Acts 2:41). A man by the gate called Beautiful was healed as Peter used the authority granted him in Christ's name, and soon the number of believers grew to about five thousand (see Acts 3:1–4:4). Demons also recognized their authority because of who walked with them, as the disciples cast out many evil spirits.

Others, like the seven sons of Sceva, tried to cast out demons using the weight of Jesus' name, but they had no influence because they had no relationship with Christ. This is why the demons attacked and humiliated them. "Jesus I know, and I know about Paul, but who are you?" was the demons' response before they shredded these men (Acts 19:15). They recognize and submit only to those who walk with Jesus. When you get saved, God writes your name in heaven in the Book of Life, and when your name is written in heaven, you can use His name on earth to set the captives free (see Luke 10:17–20).

The interesting thing is that the demons knew about Paul. He had a reputation in the heavenly realm because he was a man of prayer. Paul was by no means a spiritual gunslinger, but he definitely threw his weight around in the right place. He did not throw his weight or influence around earthly men first; he initiated it first in the heavenly places through prayer. He was known there because he walked with the Rock of Ages. From the example of Paul and the other disciples, we learn a powerful truth regarding the weight of Jesus'

> When your name is written in heaven, Jesus gives you His glorious name to write history on earth.

name and our relationship with Him. It is simply this: When your name is written in heaven, Jesus gives you His glorious name to write history on earth.

People set out the sick and demonized in hopes that Peter would walk by and the "shadow of the Almighty" (Psalm 91:1) who walked with him would bring healing and deliverance (see Acts 5:15). The apostles' intimate fellowship with God resulted in His glory being released through them. Cities and entire regions were changed because the weight of God's influence empowered the believers' Kingdom message. As a matter of fact, their influence in Ephesus was so powerful that new believers publicly burned their books on witchcraft and the thriving idol-making industry was threatened (see Acts 19:17–27).

Though the first Christ-followers had favor with both God and the masses (see Acts 2:47), the Jewish religious leaders tried to silence them from preaching about Christ. The believers' response was not acquiescence but rather an appeal to God in prayer for great boldness and for His Kingdom to be advanced through signs, miracles and wonders. As a result, the place where they prayed was literally shaken by the weight of God's glory (see Acts 4:23–31). Their prayer request to proclaim God's Word with great boldness and effectiveness was answered. The culture was changed by the influence of God's glory resting upon them. Beyond revival, societal transformation occurred because they were abandoned to God.

Revival Glory

This is not to be relegated only to the pages of the Bible. Throughout history God has used people who were totally sold out to Him.

Charles G. Finney was one of those abandoned servants of God who walked in this realm of glory during an era of revival in America. Finney was one of the most powerful preachers of the Second Great Awakening. As we see in Finney's *Revival Lectures* (Revell, 1993), an "unusual influence" would overwhelm those present in his meetings, as people became convicted of sin because of the glory of God resting upon him.

Many times the atmosphere was transformed because the "shadow of the Almighty" walked with him. On one occasion, Finney walked into a factory to see the machinery, still carrying the glory of a recent revival meeting on him. As he walked into a room full of employees, a woman began to murmur negatively about him and the revival. But when Finney turned to look at her with eyes of compassion, her countenance changed. She became sorrowful for her sins, coming under the influence of God's compassion and conviction, and wept and cried out to God. This spark released a fire that went throughout the entire factory. According to Finney, "The feeling spread throughout the establishment like fire, and in a few hours almost every person employed there was under conviction; so much so that the owner, though a worldly man, was astounded, and requested to have the works stopped and a prayer meeting held."

Most of the young factory workers were present, and many came under deep conviction. When Finney visited the factory the next morning, more than three thousand people were waiting. Because of the presence of God's glory, Finney only had to explain the Gospel briefly before they made an immediate decision for Christ. Three thousand souls were saved that day, just as in the second chapter of Acts, because Finney walked into this factory with the right Person.

This is just one example of how God used Finney, as whole regions came under the influence of the Holy Spirit so powerfully that people miles away would be touched by the manifested presence of God. Records demonstrate that Finney's revivals had such an impact on Rochester, New York, that there was no crime in that city for five years! Finney also took a strong stand against slavery, and he was instrumental in social justice by bringing societal transformation through revival. Many believe that he carried the weight of God's glory in the manner that he did because of his faith, character, integrity and prayer life.

Bringing Glory to the Workplace

Just as God used Finney, He wants to use you as well, and He is giving you an invitation to walk with Him in a new level of intimacy. If your name is written in heaven, it is God's desire to give you His name to write history on earth. Like Finney, God can specifically use you to transform the workplace.

I have a friend who is an awesome woman of faith and prayer whom God has used powerfully in the workplace as an intercessor. She was working in a corporate office when God began speaking to her about her co-workers. She started going to work early every day to pray for them. On occasion she fasted for them as well.

Doors began opening for her to share God's love with her co-workers, and they began to talk with her about their life circumstances. Some came to her office for prayer for physical ailments and were healed. Before long her office developed a reputation that she was not even aware of. She would come back from meetings or from lunch and find people sitting in her chair. She finally asked what was going on, and learned that her co-workers called her chair the "healing chair"—and would go into her office because a healing presence was here.

That presence was a Person, and Christ's influence changed the atmosphere of her work group. Believers and unbelievers alike were drawn to her office, and many lives were saved, healed and changed because of her relationship with God. God also blessed the work of their hands, as her group was among the top performers in their company. And because she proved herself to be a woman of integrity, God also gave her influence in company decisions. Her superiors held her in high regard, and her words had substance because she walked into work with the Rock of Ages.

When you go to work, does the atmosphere change when you walk into the room?

If you wholly set yourself apart and abandon yourself to God, He will use you—as a carrier of His glory—to change the atmosphere of your home, neighborhood, workplace and region. When you fellowship with God in worship, fasting and prayer, people will begin to look around and say, "Who just walked into the room?" Then you can introduce them to the influential Person you are walking with: Jesus.

Walking with the Great Physician

Another example comes from a medically documented miracle that occurred when my friend Guy Peh walked into an emergency room with the right Person. The following story about Pastor Sharon Lee, found on Guy's website (www.guypeh.com), also appeared in a Watonga, Oklahoma, newspaper, the *Watonga Republican*:

> November 6, 1999—[Pastor Sharon Lee] suffered a heart attack the morning after a Friday night revival service. That Saturday afternoon in the emergency room, Lee was without a pulse for over 30 minutes. . . . Guy Peh laid his hands [on her in the name of Jesus] and commanded her brain to be restored and that she must live. Dr. Ash, a Muslim doctor on duty during this time, was recorded in the newspaper as saying, "I was very surprised when I was told that she was coming back and had a pulse. . . . Sharon is alive with no brain damage!"

Because Guy leads a life of intimacy with God through fasting and prayer in secret, he is being used as a vessel of honor today. He walks with the Rock of Ages.

Finally, the influence and weight of God's glory can be seen in this powerful story told by my friend Barbara Wentroble in her book *Prophetic Intercession* (Renew Books, 1999).

Barbara recounts the story of an intercessor named Anna in the country of Burma who went to a certain spot in her village to pray every morning at four o'clock. Even when a Buddhist temple was built on the very spot in which she prayed, this persistent intercessor continued her early prayer time in the area.

One day the Lord spoke to her to do a prophetic act, which eventually led her to jail! As Barbara tells the story, Anna heard the Lord speak to her.

> "Take a small stone and throw it at the temple in the name of Jesus," she heard in her spirit. After finding a small stone, Anna threw it at the temple while shouting, "in the name of Jesus." At 4:00 a.m. there was no one around to see or hear what she did.

However, the temple heard! Immediately, the Buddhist temple came crumbling down. It was not long before the police came to arrest Anna. Everyone knew she came to that spot to pray every day. She had done it for years. She was a prime suspect.

"What did you do?" they questioned. She told them the truth, "I threw a small stone at the temple in the name of Jesus." The fear of the Lord fell on all the policemen. If her God caused a small stone to make a big temple fall, they didn't want to do anything to incite Him to be angry. They immediately released Anna. She had been obedient to perform a prophetic act because of the prompting of the Holy Spirit. God's power was then released, causing the police officials to see the power of almighty God, the true God!

I am not, of course, advocating vandalism. But I do want you to see the influence of the name of Jesus Christ. When we walk with the Rock of Ages and are obedient to His will, the weight of God's glory can use even a pebble and eliminate any stronghold.

Powerful!

As you can see, love, faith, the anointing and God's glory are all powerful substances that emanate from God's presence and change the atmosphere wherever they are present. All of these are made accessible because of the most powerful heavenly substance of them all: the blood of Jesus. People who have favor with the world may have the ability to move the hearts of people. But those who have favor with God—through an intimate relationship with Him that results in character and integrity—have access to influence that moves angels and dispels demons.

In the Church today, we have more affluence than ever, but what we need is more divine influence. It is one thing to be able to say, "Here is silver and gold," but it is altogether another thing to be able to say, "Rise and be healed in Jesus' name!" (see Acts 3:6). We need the power of yesterday—today! In the next chapter, we will see how influence changes culture.

EXERCISING INFLUENCE *through Prayer*

Father, thank You that You are the Rock of Ages. We praise Your glorious name! Thank You for lending Your weight, credibility and influence to us. Now, God, we ask that You would distinguish Your people from all other people on earth with Your glory. Change the atmosphere of our workplaces by the weight of Your glory. O God, invade the marketplace with Your manifest presence.

Lord, we pray for the release of signs, wonders and miracles in Your name. You are the same yesterday, today and forever. God, heal the sick, raise the dead and set the captives free—by and for Your glory. Release revival glory, and transform our cities once again.

We thank You that, by the weight of Your glory, every knee will bow and every tongue will confess that Jesus Christ is Lord. Save souls by the weight of Your glory, and may Your glory cover the earth as the waters cover the sea. Like Moses we cry, "Show us Your glory!" In Jesus' name, Amen.

Thermostats or Thermometers?

As WE SAW IN THE STORY of David, Absalom and Ahithophel, influence was very important in increasing Absalom's foothold in Israel. Though he was defeated in the end, Absalom did create a tremendous groundswell of support. In our modern times, millions of dollars are spent in order to create the kind of public sway Absalom received. The prince and power of the air used Absalom and Ahithophel as celebrities to release his influence on earth. David was God's star, however, so he prevailed even though the public was not with him. From monarchies to presidential elections, influence is the key to determining the outcome for any leader.

Gauging Intercession in America

The title of a particular movie came to mind during prayer one day: *Fahrenheit 9/11*. Suddenly the *9/11* in the title reminded me of Amos 9:11, referring to the tent, or tabernacle, of David, which I equate with God's house of prayer. After pondering this, I also thought about how *Fahrenheit* represents a range or gauge of temperature. I felt the Lord was saying to me, "For too long the Church has been a thermometer, which only reacts to the existing conditions. But I have called her to be a thermostat, which *changes* the environment. If My house will turn up the heat in prayer, I will change the atmosphere over this nation. I desire to release My influence through the praying Church to sustain future generations to come."

Christians need to pray and be involved in every realm of society (business, media, education and so on), including the political process. It is not that we want the Church to become political but rather, as Francis Frangipane says, "We are to make the political spiritual" through prayer and acts of obedience. Through prayer the will and influence of Christ's Kingdom must come to earth.

We must continue to seek the Lord in prayer, fasting and acts of intercession to change the moral climate in our nation. For too long, we have abdicated our responsibility, and this generation must pay the price now, before it costs our sons and daughters later. As quoted in *A Testament of Hope: The Essential Writings of Martin Luther King, Jr.* (HarperSanFrancisco, 1986), Dr. King said:

> There was a time when the church was very powerful. It was during that period when the early Christians rejoiced when they were deemed worthy to suffer for what they believed. In those days the church was not merely a thermometer that recorded the ideas and principles of popular opinion; it was a thermostat that transformed the mores of society.

God is requiring the "colony of heaven" (as Dr. King called us) to change the spiritual and moral climate in America through

His influence. In this chapter, we will talk about influence as the Lord spoke of it—as leaven. Leaven, or yeast, as some translate this biblical word, is an excellent metaphor to describe influence. You may recall that one of the definitions of *influence* says it is a force that alters the actions of others consciously or unconsciously. Influence is likened to an infection that permeates the environment it is in, greatly altering the end result. You will see the effects ungodly influence has had on our nation, particularly our court system. First, in order to get a better understanding, let's "bake some bread" together.

A Little Leaven in Your Lump?

One of my fondest childhood memories is of my mother baking bread. She would mix some yeast, or leaven, and a small piece of dough together and make a little ball. Then she would place this small, concentrated batch of leaven inside the dough she intended to bake. The entire mixture was set aside at room temperature before going into the oven. Yeast is a fungus that, when placed in dough, causes the entire lump to rise. The yeast releases pockets of air until it permeates the environment of the dough. My mother explained how the bread would rise because of the little bit of leaven. I would sit and stare for a few minutes, and it seemed as if nothing was happening.

Later, however, after returning from playing, I would recognize that the lump of dough was at least twice as large as it was before. My mother then baked the risen dough by placing it inside the oven. I thought the rising process was complete before then, but yeast also makes the bread grow in the oven. Under heat the leaven causes the entire dough to rise. The heat does not kill the fungus but rather increases its activity and releases more air, causing the bread to rise even more. Without any leaven, the bread will stay flat. I was amazed that a small amount of leaven could so greatly affect and alter the end result.

Influence operates in the same manner. It permeates the atmosphere it is in and consciously or unconsciously affects the thinking, actions and outcome of others. When influence, like leaven, is under fire, it rises and causes the existing environment to change radically. That is why Jesus told this brief parable: "The kingdom of heaven is like yeast that a woman took and mixed into a large amount of flour until it worked all through the dough" (Matthew 13:33).

Christ's Kingdom influence may seem insignificant, like a small portion of leaven. When godly influence is in an environment, it may appear that nothing is happening. But people's minds and actions are being affected. Sometimes the results will not be recognized until years later, as some plant, others water and God brings the increase. Yet, instead of dying under the fire of change and persecution, godly influence expands—increasing all the more.

When the Jews were under Roman occupation, for example, they expected the Messiah to come with a violent sword and overthrow the government. But He came instead with a cross and released an influential love that transformed the world. Rome went from persecuting Christians to years later declaring itself to be a Christian empire, when Constantine became emperor. Most thought that Christianity would dissipate under the fire of persecution, but on the contrary, God's Kingdom advanced all the more.

There are also, however, influences or leavens from the kingdom of darkness that, if left unchecked, will increase and corrode an environment and eventually a culture. As we see in the book of Exodus, the Israelites left Egypt in haste, eating unleavened bread—which represents how we are to flee the influence of the world system. The Bible says that "one sinner destroys much good" (Ecclesiastes 9:18) and "bad company corrupts good character" (1 Corinthians 15:33). In other words, the wrong friends and associates will, over time, negatively influence your thinking and behavior.

Paul also wrote twice that "a little leaven leavens the whole lump" (1 Corinthians 5:6; Galatians 5:9 NASB). Referring to the influence of sexual immorality, Paul was telling the Corinthians to monitor the environment they placed themselves in—because eventually it will corrupt you. As the older generation used to say, "If you lie down with dogs, you will get up with fleas."

Jesus spoke of a number of different yeasts or leavens, representing influence, that His followers need to beware of: the influence of the Pharisees and the Sadducees (see Matthew 16:5–12; Luke 12:1) and the influence of Herod (see Mark 8:15). In addition to all of these influences being referred to by the Lord as hypocrisy, there are notable characteristics to each of them: for the Pharisees, legalism; for the Sadducees, unbelief; and for Herod, a sensual, worldly spirit that sought political clout.

We also need to beware of the leavens of malice and wickedness (see 1 Corinthians 5:8). Based on the issues the apostle Paul addressed in 1 Corinthians, we can see how these things crept into the Corinthian church. He knew these negative influences have the potential of destroying congregations and society. Paul realized that even though the majority were not committing these sins, eventually everyone could be affected by a sustained spiritual atmosphere created by sinful leaven. Remember, influence operates best unconsciously and undetected, and it permeates when unaddressed.

Paul knew the Corinthian believers did not realize that their mindsets were being subtly corrupted and their spiritual lives were being drained due to tolerating sin in their midst. He understood, conversely, that when churches cultivate the spiritual environment through holiness, prayer, worship and acts of obedience, someone can come under the influence of God's love and unconsciously be affected by God's presence. People become convicted of sin, desire God and His Kingdom and want to live for Him. Paul understood the blessings and curses of influence. He knew the question is not "Are you being influenced?" but rather "What is influencing you?"

Once influences of legalistic self-righteousness or sinful wickedness are released, they can change an entire culture. You have probably sensed cultural differences in visiting various cities. Think of the difference between being in New Orleans during Mardi Gras, which is a pageantry of sin, and being in Pasadena during the Rose Bowl parade with its appeal to families. Negative cultural influences will also be reflected in the media, arts, literature and other expressions, and they eventually affect laws governing society. How is this evil leaven restrained?

> The Church, as the salt of the earth, is meant to be the restraining force that negates the leaven of the enemy. But if we lose our flavor, the enemy's influence, instead of the Church's, will leaven society

Experienced bakers, whether they are making pizza or bread, have a secret weapon when working with leaven or yeast. Can you guess what it is? Salt! I have been told that sometimes the dough rises too fast when there is too much yeast. In order to restrain the fermenting of the yeast, bakers add salt to the dough. If the salt has no flavor, however, it will not keep the yeast from affecting the dough. In like manner, the Church, as the salt of the earth, is meant to be the restraining force that negates the leaven of the enemy. But if we lose our flavor, the enemy's influence, instead of the Church's, will leaven society (see Matthew 5:13). You see, influence—whether good or evil—shapes and transforms culture.

From Atmospheres to Cultures

Influence is the vital element for societal transformation of any type—for good *or* evil purposes. Within a society, influence is the leaven that affects an environment—and herein lies its impact. First, influence from the unseen realm, whether good or bad, must be released through a human agent on earth. That influence, sustained over a period of time, produces an atmosphere.*

Changing the Atmosphere

The definition of the word *atmosphere* is "a surrounding influence; a mental or moral environment; a physical milieu viewed as having a mental or moral influence." You have probably felt this in situations where anger was released and, as we say, "The atmosphere was so thick you could almost cut it with a knife." Or if you walk into an atmosphere of joy, where everyone is happy, you might start smiling unconsciously because you are under the influence of the joy in the atmosphere.

In this initial phase, attitudes are formed and feelings are experienced. Atmospheres set attitudes that, once sustained, are very powerful—either negatively or positively. In one city, for example, Jesus could not do many miracles because of the atmosphere of unbelief, whereas in other places, He healed many because of the atmosphere of faith (see Matthew 13:58; Mark 2:1–5). The bottom line is that atmosphere surrounds influence and, when sustained over a period of time, produces a climate.

*I learned this concept from Tudor Bismark. His audio series "Dimensions, Atmospheres, and Climates" is available at https://www.tudorbismark.org/index .cfm/PageID/495/index.html. The discussion given here regarding the effects of atmospheres or climates grew out of talks I had with my mentor and good friend Pastor Dutch Sheets.

143

Climates, Seeds and Moods

Climate is defined as "the prevailing temper, outlook and set of attitudes or environmental conditions characterizing a group or period." The experiences in the climate and the set of environmental attitudes, good or bad, create a mood. The mood of the climate births ideas, as revelation is released in the form of precepts. Precepts, or seed logic, produce ideas, thoughts and revelation that set the prevailing expectation for things to happen in the environment.

Words are spiritual seeds, and just as seeds from certain fruit species (like bananas and pineapples) grow only in certain climates, seeds of righteousness or unrighteousness will grow only when the spiritual climate is conducive to its existence. It is not hard to predict what will happen if you are in certain climates long enough. There are certain things you expect to happen in a dark, sultry nightclub, for example, and there are certain things you expect to happen in a church worship service.

We can see why supporting and sustaining the mood of a climate is best accomplished by music. According to researchers, music is the only channel of influence that affects the right and left brain without resistance. If you heard someone sing, "The best part of waking up . . ." you most likely would reply, "is Folgers in your cup!" Chances are you have unconsciously rehearsed this jingle in the back of your mind. You can filter out conversations, movies, what you read and so on, but not music; it stays in your subconscious. Marketers spend millions of dollars on jingles for this very reason. Through fifteen to thirty seconds of music, they believe they can get their product into your mind and influence what you buy.

In addition to setting the mood, music invokes either positive or negative attributes. Since God inhabits the praises of His people, when He comes in response to Christian worship music, He brings the attributes of His Kingdom with Him: love, healing, holiness, forgiveness, security and so on. Unfortunately, Satan inhabits the praises of his people as well and releases the demonic attributes of his dark kingdom through music: hatred, lust, death, insecurity and so on. Music is important to the release of revelation during this phase.

This climate will grip your attention as delights begin to determine desires. Sooner or later, people will desire to manifest the attributes and characteristics of the climate, based on who or what they are worshiping. What they behold is what they become, as they become like what or whom they are listening to. People who listen to hip hop gangsta rapper "50 Cent" will have thoughts of doing drive-by shootings. People who listen to Karen Wheaton and Judy Jacobs want to save the lost. People who stay under the climate of Marilyn Manson's music will have suicidal thoughts, whereas people who listen to Jason Upton and Michael W. Smith will desire freedom and more of Jesus. Music is important to reinforcing the precepts of a society.

For some people, hip hop music (which I do not endorse) is more than an art form—it is a way of life. As demonstrated by G. Craige Lewis (www.exministries.com), hip hop music has become an established subculture, influenced by its religious origins. The Temple of Hip Hop is an esoteric Afrocentric—rather than Christocentric—religion, replete with a mixture of Islam, Rastafarianism and other religions. Because these hip hop artists put their "doctrine" in their music, their fans' clothes, hairstyles, manner of speech (slang) and so on are manifestations describing their lifestyles and philosophic values.

The influence a musician can have on a culture is amazing. A nuclear physicist from MIT can say "No more nukes" and get no response from a crowd, but a third-grade-dropout rock music celebrity can say "No more nukes" and fifty thousand people will chant hysterically along with him! Music and musicians, whether dark or light, are important to sustaining spiritual climates in regions and eras. Fellow parents, you see why we must monitor what music and other media our children are exposed to. We must establish the right spiritual climate in our homes.

Not just music but art, movies, video games and other entertainment media set the climatic moods for homes, cities, regions and age groups. They even mark eras of time—the Roaring Twenties, for instance, or the hippie movement that is synonymous with the 1960s. As you can see, once climates are prolonged, things become predictable and tendencies develop. That is why climates, good or bad, sustained over a period of time produce a belief system.

Belief Systems and Tendencies

A *belief system* can be defined as "a habit of mind influenced by a pattern of related forces or attractions." During this phase, precepts are turned into concepts in which ideas and experiences are connected. Are the ideologies you learn important? You bet! As important as what you learn, however, is whom you learn ideologies from and the spiritual climate in which you are educated.

Teachers have powerful influence because they help shape the worldview through which we interpret life experiences. A Christian teaching science can, by his or her godly influence, lecture in a way that causes children to stand in awe of the God of creation, whereas an atheist teaching science can lecture in a manner that causes children to lean on their own understanding, absent of God's involvement.

A belief system will eventually operate through your subconscious and affect what you do instinctively. If you were bitten by a snake in a wooded climate in the past, for example, the first thing you might do if you see a three-foot-long squiggly thing in the forest now is jump back. After jumping back, you may consciously say, "Let's see what this is. It looks like a snake, but it's really a rope." You responded the way you did, of course, because of your experiential knowledge and belief system that says, "Beware of squiggly things in the woods." Rather than responding to present truth, you were reacting to experiential knowledge. Understanding a person's belief system will reveal why that person accepts what he or she believes is truth.

This is a very important phase, because what you believe shapes what you think, and consequently, what you think determines your attitudes and actions. Prolonged beliefs eventually result in behavioral tendencies that develop a pattern, which becomes accepted as normal. This is why a belief system, sustained over time, produces a stronghold.

Strongholds and Accepted Norms

A *stronghold* is "a fortified place; a place of security or survival; a place dominated by a particular group or marked by a particular characteristic." A negative stronghold is a fortified belief system that exalts itself against the knowledge of God (see 2 Corinthians 10:3–5). Ed Silvoso, in his book *That None Should Perish* (Regal, 1994), defines a *stronghold* as "a mindset impregnated with hopelessness that causes us to accept as unchangeable situations that we know are contrary to the will of God." Such a mindset concedes, "This is the way it will always be; things will never change." People accept conditions in life, even horribly abusive conditions, as normal.

Biblically speaking, strongholds can be either evil or good. David stated that the Lord was the "stronghold" of his life (Psalm 27:1). So a stronghold can be a fortified belief system that supports the knowledge of God. Examining strongholds reveals a person's view of God, family values and other social issues. Whether good or bad, a stronghold essentially creates an accepted norm. What we accept as normal, however, may not be the correct standard of function or the way things are supposed to be. A person can live in an environment of abnormality for so long that dysfunction becomes the accepted norm. I can illustrate this with a humorous example of my own "normal abnormality" as I was growing up.

When I was a teenager, I lost the key to my bedroom door and locked myself out of my room. I took the screws out of the door handle and removed the doorknob, exposing a round hole. If I closed the door completely, I could not reopen it, because there was no handle or doorknob to open it. So I improvised. I used a butter knife from the kitchen to open the door by placing the knife inside the exposed latch area and turning it like a doorknob. (Don't laugh at me; you have probably done it yourself!)

This practice would have been appropriate for a few days, but it lasted for several months. I learned to remember not to close the door all the way. It was always propped open. I did not ask my parents to fix the door because I was embarrassed about losing my key. My behavior, therefore, became the accepted norm. All I had to do was get someone to replace the doorknob and buy new keys, but I did not want anyone to know I had lost my keys. I chose to function in abnormality, because shame was my stronghold. I placed butter knives in my room just in case the door was closed tightly. I kept one on top of the doorframe on the entry side, just in case my brother or sisters closed the door.

Let's suppose my friends wanted to play basketball with my ball but it was behind the closed door of my room. Imagine the fix I would be in if there was no butter knife because someone had removed it from my secret hiding place. Due to my embarrassment, I would not want to get a knife to open the door in front of everyone. So I would probably tell them to find another ball or play without me. I functioned in abnormality for so long that butter knives became keys, which seemed more logical than replacing the doorknob.

While my story is humorous, it shows how something becomes an accepted norm and helps explain why people accept certain living conditions. On a more serious note, this is why some women who have been battered by their husbands for years stay in those relationships. They have functioned in abnormality for so long that they believe their husbands hit them because they love them. It sounds strange—and sad—but it is true. As you can see, just as a butter knife can become a key, good can become evil and evil can become good when sustained abnormal conditions become the accepted norm.

This can be broadened beyond individual and personal application. The term *stronghold* also describes the philosophical and behavioral norms of regions and nations, especially politically. Why are some regions and states in our country considered Republican strongholds and others are labeled Democratic strongholds? Because the differing ideologies have been sustained so long that a certain way of thinking and voting in the region has been accepted as normal. Beyond politics, of course, you can see how this principle applies to cities, regions and nations. Consequently, this is why a stronghold, sustained over a period of time, produces a culture.

Culture and Way of Life

A *culture* is defined as "the body of customary beliefs, social forms and material traits constituting a distinct complex of tradition of a racial, religious or social group." The word *culture* originally referred to the art or practice of "cultivating," in relation to farming. (*Agriculture* means "field cultivation.") Seeds are tilled or cultivated in environmental conditions, causing growth and producing healthy fruit.

Influence, likewise, is sown and then cultivated, or cultured, in the environmental conditions in which it best grows. Atmospheric conditions, spiritual climates and belief systems all till the soil, so to speak. As a result, influence is able to be cultivated into ideas, which then grow into strongholds. The growth process continues until behaviors that are the fruitful characteristics of a culture are manifested. The culture then describes an established way of life.

Now remember, all of this began with influence that incubated and eventually permeated the entire society. As you can see, the actions and behaviors of people in cultures reflect the persistence of strongholds, belief systems, climates and atmospheres established by sustained spiritual influence. Consciously or unconsciously, that influence, which comes from either the kingdom of darkness or the Kingdom of light, will influence government.

The Court's Influence on Culture

Beginning in the 1960s, the progressive effects of influence from the kingdom of darkness can be seen in America's Supreme Court. During the '60s, this nation went through a leavening process in her court system. Unfortunately, that ungodliness incubated and is still influencing our culture today.

In 1961 influential leaven from the kingdom of darkness came into the Supreme Court of our nation in the form of *Torcaso v. Watkins*, in which the court ruled that secular humanism is a recognized religion. Most people ignored the ruling, but the enemy gained legal ground through human agents to release a spiritual influence that claimed we are our own gods. That influence was sustained, creating an atmosphere of hostility toward God. After all, if humanism says we are god, then who needs to pray? And the next year, that is precisely what we stopped doing.

In the 1962 *Engel v. Vitale* case, the Supreme Court ruled, through the influence of a few, that organized prayer must be taken out of public schools. The simple prayer that was abolished was, "Almighty God, we acknowledge our dependence upon Thee, and we beg Thy blessings upon us, our parents, our teachers and our country." A prayer spoken by 39 million children and 2 million teachers was taken away, affecting the climate of our nation and the protection of its leaders.

In 1963, the year after the prayer covering was lifted, President John Kennedy was assassinated. Chaos ensued, and the fire of change produced a climate of radical unbelief. Rock music groups became the voice of a generation that found itself led into drug experimentation, false religions and the occult. The Beatles cried out "Help!" but the Church did not answer the call. As the world was looking for answers, the Church—the "salt of the earth"—was looking for the Rapture! Influenced by a pharisaic mindset, the cold and legalistic "salt" lost its flavor. The Church checked out of society, thus squandering her godly influence.

Turned off by hypocrisy in the Church, a generation sought personal gratification as an opiate to anesthetize its pain. The hippie movement was born. Teachers such as Timothy Leary aided this belief system. A reckless abandonment for peace, love and meaning—void of pursuing God—resulted in the sexual revolution. Pleasure became the accepted norm for living, and self became the stronghold.

An unspoken philosophy ruled our nation, creating a fortified logic that said, "In order to sustain pleasure for self, and since humanism says we are god, we can't have interference. We don't need children, therefore; they just get in the way. Besides, who wants to bring a child into this world today?" God does, because that is how He always changes a generation—through offspring. "To us a child is born, to us a son is given" (Isaiah 9:6).

Nonetheless, the final stamp came in 1973, when abortion became law. The landmark *Roe v. Wade* Supreme Court decision has marked our society as a culture of death. Many believe this is a hopeless situation. But with God all things are possible! We can change the prevailing influence of our nation through intercession and action.

The shift to turn America back in the right direction must come through this generation. We are called to influence society through the weapon of prayer, tearing down demonic thoughts and pretenses through obedient acts that counter this worldly culture. Read how *The Message* describes our spiritual warfare in 2 Corinthians 10:3–5:

> The world is unprincipled. It's dog-eat-dog out there! The world doesn't fight fair. But we don't live or fight our battles that way—never have and never will. The tools of our trade aren't for marketing or manipulation, but they are for demolishing that entire massively corrupt culture. We use our powerful God-tools for smashing warped philosophies, tearing down barriers erected against the truth of God, fitting every loose thought and emotion and impulse into the structure of life shaped by Christ.

From this we understand our call to governmental intercession. Today some philosophies need smashing and some thought barriers need to be torn down. The enemy has influenced our modern culture long enough. The praying Church can shift the spiritual climate of our nation. Remember, we have history on our side. Slavery and segregation came to an end because of the prayer and sacrifice of God's remnant. Now God is looking for a remnant who would dare to believe that the giant strongholds of our generation can come down. He is looking for Christians who will join in intercession and change our cultural influences through prayer—so radically that abortion becomes an absurdity and every life is valued!

This can happen if we become thermostats and pray until the atmosphere is changed. But we cannot stop there.

Sustaining Prayer and Intercession

We must persist in prayer, worship and intercession until atmospheric conditions birth climates that are sustained until the Kingdom of God influences modern culture. Many times we will change the atmosphere, but we do not sustain it until the climate and other phases are formed. Consequently, things go back to where they were before, or seven times worse than before (see Matthew 12:45). This is why houses of prayer are important and why united, citywide prayer groups are arising. People all over America are committing to sustained prayer and intercession.

Several years ago, a group of intercessors gathered to pray at an abortion clinic in Chattanooga, Tennessee. They had no picket signs, only intercession. One of the intercessors had a dream and convinced the group they needed to take Communion in front of the abortion clinic. Prayer warriors from around the city, in a united effort, carried out this prayer assignment for almost two years. In the natural, it looked as if nothing was happening. But as they did this, they were sustaining something that affected the atmosphere spiritually. Eventually the climate over the abortion clinic changed, and people stopped going to it. Ultimately it went into bankruptcy. Five pastors found out about this and pooled their resources together and bought the facility. They turned it into a crisis pregnancy center with a memorial in the back to aborted babies.

This happened because a group of people became thermostats that sustained an atmosphere in prayer—an atmosphere, which became a climate, which then became a belief system, which then tore down a stronghold of despair. And in its place a crisis pregnancy center has become a stronghold of hope! These saints released a fragrant aroma through intercession that advanced the culture of the Kingdom of heaven.

Church, we have functioned in abnormality for too long in this nation. We do not have to accept things contrary to God's standard and call evil good and good evil. Why are we settling for butter knives when through prayer our Father has given us keys (see Isaiah 22:22; Matthew 16:19)? Through sustained intercession, we can open the door to God's promises and shut the door to negative influences in our cities.

We have been thermometers long enough; let's be thermostats! This generation must dare to believe and turn up the heat in the house of prayer. Let's sustain intercession, become thermostats and change the mores of society.

Imagine it: Through sustained prayer, Kingdom joy can create a new atmosphere in our homes and communities. Worship songs can give us a heavenly climate, replacing the dirge of death our children receive in hip hop, rock and today's pop music. Prayer and teaching about Creation can come back into our schools—giving us a belief system that does not lean on its own Darwinian understanding but rather stands in awe of God. God can be our stronghold and replace the fortress of dysfunction in our society. A culture of death can be replaced by a heavenly Kingdom culture, placing value on eternal life, and every life, forevermore.

EXERCISING INFLUENCE *through Prayer*

Father, I choose to function no longer in abnormality and half-baked religion that settles for butter knives when You

have given us keys of authority. Give me wisdom, reve-
lation and discernment, and expose sinful influences that
need to be removed from my life. In the name of Jesus, I
shut the door to demonic leaven in my home. I ask that
Your influence would come and be sustained in my life.

I open the door to You, King of Glory, that my way
of life may reflect the culture of Your Kingdom. Sustain
Your influence in my life, that I may be an influence for
You at work, in my neighborhood and in my city—until
everything in my sphere of influence is leavened by the
power of Your love.

O God, use me as salt to restrain and negate the enemy's
influence! Your Church is tired of being the thermometer
and adjusting to the conditions around us. God, we ask,
release the fire of holiness and make us Your thermostat.

Now, Lord, I join with Your Church in praying for re-
vival at our colleges and universities. Lord, in America
many of these institutions were founded as Christian col-
leges that raised up godly leaders. But, Father, today the
Tree of the Knowledge of Good and Evil has caused us
to lean on our own understanding. Lord, we confess that
our sin and its fruit have raised up many godless leaders
who have become lawyers, legislators and judges helping
to produce a culture of death. Lord, turn up the heat of
passion in the house of prayer, we cry, and raise up fervent
prayer warriors at every school!

O God, release a revival of prayer on campuses until a
revival of souls takes place. Change the atmosphere at our
universities from one of doubt to one of belief and faith in
You. Make our schools places of worship for Your name's
sake again. May good seed, planted by godly parents and
teachers, take root and grow. Great Teacher, instead of see-
ing professors leaning on their own understanding, please

shift the belief systems of faculties until people stand in awe of the living God.

Lord, tear down ideological strongholds of hopelessness and despair in our colleges and universities, and make them strongholds for the living God again. We ask, Lord, that You raise up a new breed of intellectuals like the apostle Paul. Give us judges as at the first and lawyers as at the beginning. Father, use them to shift the influence in our courts and break off humanistic ideologies in our nation until it reflects the culture of Your Kingdom! In Jesus' name, Amen.

8

Influence and Our Offspring

GOD ONCE GAVE ME AN INCREDIBLE DREAM about the dreamer Dr. Martin Luther King Jr. I had this dream, ironically, the night before I was to speak at Dr. King's historic church, Dexter Avenue Baptist Church in Montgomery, Alabama—where the civil rights movement began. I was there at the request of my dear friend Lou Engle. In the dream, Lou and I were driving to Dexter Avenue Baptist, but we could not get there without picking up Dr. King. As we pulled up to his house, Dr. King came out with a white duffel bag with black handles. He went to the curb and dumped out everything in the duffel bag, and once it was empty, surprisingly, he threw away the bag as well. He then walked over to our SUV and opened the door to ride with us. In the dream, I thought his bag would make a nice souvenir. But when I went to retrieve it, Dr. King grabbed me and abruptly turned me around. Putting his hands on my shoulders, he stared intently into my eyes and said, "No! Do not go back and pick that up." With that the dream ended.

When I awoke, I knew this dream was significant. While praying for the interpretation, the Lord had me focus on the vehicle, which represents ministries or movements. Next, emphasis was placed on the white duffel bag with black handles. The black handles represented my race, African Americans, and the white duffel bag represented my "white baggage." The dream revealed how God wanted me, as an African American, to "handle" any unresolved white issues. The Lord was saying to me, *Empty yourself of any residue of unforgiveness, bitterness and resentment. Get rid of your "white baggage," and ride in the new movement that will bring revival and justice to everyone.*

The New Justice Movement

I shared this dream at Dexter Avenue Baptist the next evening, and we had a powerful time of repentance and racial reconciliation. The questions before us all are "Do I have any racial baggage? If I do, what color is it?" Whatever color it is, get rid of it—and get in the new justice movement.

Today we have the opportunity to partner with God and influence heaven and earth the same way He did in the civil rights movement. What is this new justice movement about? It is about the civil rights of the unborn. One cold winter day, God confirmed this to me in a powerful way.

I was at a prayer meeting in Washington, D.C., which was celebrating Martin Luther King Jr. Day that year on January 17, 2005. The prayer meeting was held at the Dirksen Building, the place where the Senate Judiciary Committee meets. This committee is critical because it conducts hearings pertaining to the President's choices for Supreme Court justices and federal court of appeals judges. During this prayer gathering, I had an encounter with God that has changed my life forever.

While in worship, I felt a deep pain coming from the depths of my soul. An issue I had dealt with years before suddenly came to the surface. I was somewhat bewildered, since I had forgiven myself and the other person who was involved. I had mourned with sinful regret over what I had done. I even had pastors pray and lead me to spiritual freedom regarding this issue. But God was taking me to another layer of deep healing and closure.

As a young Christian, I had made a commitment to sexual purity before marriage. But instead, I sold out to temporary pleasure. This major setback in my walk with God cost me years of painful memories. I realize that I made a decision to sin, but I had help. No, the devil did not make me do it, but neither was he an innocent bystander. I had assistance. Looking back, I realize I was under the influence of one of the major spirits of this age.

In this chapter, we will talk about this Jezebelic influence and its deceptive impact on our nation. We will see how a united generational effort must combat this system that seeks governmental control. I will also finish sharing the details of my story and how God is using this area of my life to heal others and save lives. But first we must understand how influence and deception work together.

Before Your Very Eyes

Daniel 8:25, which refers to a future ruler, says that "he will cause deceit to succeed by his influence" (NASB). That intrigues me. The Antichrist is going to use influence to make his deception work. Now, deception alone is pretty powerful. After all, when you are right you know it, and when you are wrong you know it. But when you are deceived, you have no clue! Nonetheless, deception works best to affect your actions subconsciously and unknowingly when it is coupled with the subtle power of influence.

One example is a sleight-of-hand artist. I once heard a professional magician talk about the influence of laughter. He said that when an audience is under the influence of laughter, a magician can get away with doing a deceptive trick without their knowledge. He explained that laughter causes the brain to let down its defenses, and that we cannot laugh and think at the same time. Scripture affirms that laughter and cheer are even good for us medicinally (see Proverbs 17:22). Dentists use nitrous oxide, better known as "laughing gas," for this very reason, so that their patients are not aware of minor pain or injections. Under the influence of laughter, however, we do not process logic, and our cognition is relaxed. As a result, magicians are able to switch or exchange things without our knowledge. Sleight-of-hand artists are able to make their deception work by influence.

In similar manner, influence in the hands of the enemy—whether through laughter or any other channel—is used to break down your defenses in order to get you to accept lies. The enemy has used laughter like an anesthetic to inject us with his deception, especially through television. Think about it. Through sitcoms we have laughed our way into accepting lies about homosexuality, adultery and premarital sex as cultural norms. It is hard to believe that not long ago homosexuality was listed medically as a psychological disorder. Now it is no longer included in the abnormal psychology textbooks, and homophobia has become a psychological disorder! While we have been laughing at our TVs, the devil has been laughing at us—as his sleight of hand is changing our values right under our noses.

Of course, laughter is only one method of influence used by the enemy. The spirit behind this pursues every societal channel of influence in order to spread its perverted and immoral ideology and seeks to infiltrate the Church in order to destroy cautious

her. It also uses affluence to make its deceptive influence work. The spirit I am talking about is the spirit of Jezebel. We see this method of operation in both the Old and New Testaments, legalizing injustice in 1 Kings 21 and leading believers into sexual immorality in the book of Revelation.

Jezebel's System

Jezebel was the wife of King Ahab of Israel. She was from a foreign nation, and God had forbidden the Israelites to intermarry with people from other nations. Nonetheless, foolish Ahab married Jezebel. She used the influence gained by her relationship with King Ahab to establish her native Baal worship, a form of witchcraft, in Israel. The ultimate desire of the spirit of Jezebel is governmental rule. This spirit attempts to snuff out any godly environment over a territory, city, region or nation and replace it with a demonic atmosphere. This is done to create a culture that reflects the values of the kingdom of darkness.

Queen Jezebel attempted to accomplish this in Israel by taking out the people who leavened society: "the school of the prophets." She killed prophets in order to destroy their teaching of the history of God's faithfulness in the nation. Today her spirit does this by taking over education in order to root out the knowledge of God in public schools, colleges and universities.

In 1 Kings 21, we find the story of Naboth's vineyard, which shows how Jezebel used deception and influence systematically. This pattern is still used today in making deception effective through influence. First, Jezebel takes control of the media. She does this by sending out newsletters, the form of mass communication in that day. These newsletters were probably telling people her "spin" of her husband's account with Naboth. In this manner, she spreads her way of thinking, her ideology. Next, she says she needs two scoundrels to lie, claiming that

Naboth cursed both God and the king—a violation worthy of death by stoning in Israel (see Leviticus 24:15–16). Perhaps she used her money and affluence to persuade these men with payoffs. Nonetheless, to ensure that all of this would work, she does something else very unusual: Jezebel calls for a fast. But why did she do so?

For one thing, Jezebel likely was trying to create the impression that a catastrophe threatened the people that could be turned aside only if they would humble themselves before God and remove any person whose sin had brought His judgment on them. And remember, Jezebel was a Baal-worshiping witchcraft practitioner. So she is not fasting and praying to the God of Israel. She is fasting to gain influence from demonic powers in order to make her deception work!

And that is exactly what happens. She successfully uses her influence to affect the judicial system. Because of Jezebel's affluent status and demonic spiritual influence gained through occult powers, the elders and nobles who live in Naboth's city believe the false witness of these two liars. As a result, they stone Naboth to death. Although Naboth lost his life and his inheritance, he did not lose his dignity or godly influence. His resistance to the powers of darkness was important in influencing Jezebel's downfall. His sacrifice did not go unnoticed by God.

From this we see that, in addressing Jezebel, we are not dealing with just a pretty witch with makeup but an ageless spirit-being that seeks societal dominion. This spirit operated through Ahab's wife in Israel in the Old Testament and through someone else in the Church in John's Revelation in the New Testament.

In Revelation 2:20, the risen Christ says to the church in Thyatira, "Nevertheless, I have this against you: You tolerate that woman Jezebel, who calls herself a prophetess. By her teaching she misleads my servants into sexual immorality and the eating of food sacrificed to idols." Jezebel introduces compromise into the church, through sexual immorality, knowing that if she can get it into the church, she can have a field day in the world. She makes an alliance with the church, knowing that if God's moral agent docs not restrain her, she can spread her immorality throughout society. She then will turn against the church if it does not accept her perverted teaching.

In other words, what we have is a Jezebelic system designed to uproot God's Kingdom from society. Just as she persecuted the school of the prophets, today this spirit attempts to take over education to rid our history books of any reference to God. Just as she took control of the political and judicial systems in order to ensure Naboth's demise, today this spirit has influenced our judicial system to legalize abortion and same-sex marriage and to protect pornography.

Just as Jezebel took over the media to advance her way of thinking in Israel, today this system bombards our culture with Jezebel's twisted, immoral ideology. Just as she did with Naboth, the spirit of Jezebel systematically uses the economic system to bankroll her agenda in an attempt to seize our godly inheritance for her own selfish gain. She will work all channels of influence (politics, education, judicial system, media and marketplace) until all of these streams, like water, rise to become one system that covers a whole nation and erodes the Kingdom of God.

If left unattended, this spirit will ultimately strip away any grip the Church has on society. How? By getting a grip herself on the Church. That was Jezebel's purpose in Revelation, and that is her strategy today. She gets the Church to participate in her agenda. Church leaders will even endorse compromise as a result of their agreement with this spirit.

Change can come through a holy remnant, however. When the enemy comes in like a flood, the Lord will raise up a standard against him. There is hope, but victory will not come without conflict. It will take holiness, prophetic prayers, apostolic decrees and great resolve to dry up these waters. This obviously is not something that comes down because of one prayer meeting. It is the zeal of the Lord, in us, that will accomplish this—by confronting the system.

We must commit to sustained prayer that will influence generations to come. Like Naboth, this may cost us our lives, but we must resist these powers for the sake of our inheritance and for the sake of future generations. The battle will not be won overnight, and it must be a multigenerational fight. This is exactly what Elijah initiated to take this demonic system down. The real challenge is changing the spiritual conditions and environment in which Jezebel exists and rules.

Resisting the Powers

Remember, influence is likened, as a viral infection, to influenza. Even with our modern technology, scientists have not figured out how to kill the cold germ or the virus that causes the flu. One method used to stop the flu germ from spreading in your body, however, is changing the environment in which the flu exists. Viral infections force your body to produce mucus in order to have an atmosphere in which to live and spread. Doctors fight these infections by giving medicine to their patients that dries up the mucus, thus destroying the environmental conditions conducive to the virus's survival in your body. In other words, they kill the virus by killing its atmosphere. The same principle works in the spiritual realm.

Like the cold or flu virus, demon spirits cannot be killed, though we have authority over them. With our Christ-given authority, we can bind them, and we can even cast them out, but if the environmental mindset has not been transformed, then spiritual conditions can become worse than they were before (see Matthew 12:45). Countless times we pray to take out a demonic force, which is good, but an additional strategy must be employed. What we must do is change the atmospheric conditions so radically that we make it hard for Satan's Jezebelic "influenza" to exist any longer. Through prayer and prophetic action, we must dry up the environment in which this demonic influence grows (in your home, city, region, etc.) until Jezebel cannot infect others with her sick way of thinking.

In essence, we continue changing the atmosphere until her slimy influence dries up! When her ideology becomes absurd to others, Jezebel's system will begin to choke and suffocate, because the atmospheric conditions are no longer conducive for her existence and rule. This happens when godly influence, the only antidote, becomes the healing agent of the culture. Then Jezebel's influence will stop spreading, because more people become immune to her system of logic.

> Through our Kingdom authority, we resist the enemy and kill the environment where darkness rules. We must press in like Elijah did and change the atmosphere.

Through our Kingdom authority, we resist the enemy and kill the environment where darkness rules. We must press in like Elijah did and change the atmosphere.

The prophet Elijah prayed for the heavens to be shut up for three and a half years, and God answered his prayer for no rain (see 1 Kings 17:1; 18:1; James 5:17). What did this accomplish? Jezebel's main source of commerce, agriculture, was destroyed because of the drought. The demonic kingdom could no longer use Israel's natural resources to support itself. With the nation in a drought, Jezebel could no longer use Israel's land to feed her system. Through Elijah, God was basically killing her atmosphere in order to dry up her influence!

Jezebel's pocketbook was attacked, affecting her affluence, and people began to wonder about her rule. People stopped saying, "Well, we may have Baal instead of the Lord, but things are great financially. It's the economy, stupid." They began to doubt Israel's alliance with Baal worship because of Baal's lack of ability to provide. This created a sense of desperation for the God who answers prayer: Jehovah Jireh. As a result, people like Naboth were no longer bound by fear of Jezebel and Ahab, and they began to resist the powers.

Later, when Elijah called down fire from heaven, he was stopping the spread of Baal's knowledge by killing hundreds of prophets of Baal who were expanding Jezebel's influence (see 1 Kings 18:18–19, 40). This took out her education system. In the process, he called Israel back to righteousness by reminding her of God's covenant with her (see 1 Kings 18:36–39). The atmosphere began to shift, and a new generation was raised up who were not afraid of Jezebel nor enamored by her power. Fewer people were agreeing with her logic, because the climate had changed over the nation.

Several years passed, and the new king whom Elijah anointed to take the place of Ahab and Jezebel's evil son Joram took over. Zealous Jehu, along with the next generation, was able to throw Jezebel down (literally!—see 2 Kings 9:30–33) because he was not bound by her influence. You see, Naboth's sacrifice was a seed that released a godly influence affecting Jehu's generation. Surely they had heard Elijah tell of Naboth's stand against these demonic powers and how he gave his life for justice.

In Naboth's honor, Jehu threw Joram's dead body in the field that was taken from Naboth (see 2 Kings 9:24–26), because Jehu had a godly belief system that valued the history of God's faithfulness. God did not forget Naboth's resistance but used it to influence the next generation. And as a result of Elijah's stand at God's showdown with Baal, God became the strong-hold in Israel again. A Kingdom culture eventually emerged again in Israel, as Jehu became ruler instead of the family of Ahab and Jezebel.

Margaret Sanger

Today America has come under the spell of Jezebelic influence. This influence, which has gripped our thinking through media outlets, has robbed us of our godly inheritance and taken the life of our offspring. By way of TV shows, music and other channels of influence, dark powers have influenced us to accept lies regarding the life of the unborn. Though many have not operated in blatant witchcraft as Jezebel did, demonic powers are still manipulating things behind the scenes, granting affluence to those who will influence earthly representatives in order to make their deception work. This is precisely what happened with abortion and one person the enemy used to prepare the environment for the propagation of abortion in America: Margaret Sanger.

Sanger, a wealthy and powerful woman who lived from 1879 to 1966, was a eugenicist. (*Eugenics* is defined as "a science that deals with the improvement, as by control of human mating, of hereditary qualities of a race or breed.") Like Hitler and other eugenicists, she felt that the poor of all races were a drain on humankind and so these weaker "dysgenic" people should be eliminated.

According to George Grant's book, *Grand Illusions: The Legacy of Planned Parenthood* (Wolgemuth and Hyatt, 1988), Sanger was an upper-class, sophisticated racist who believed that "inferior races" were "human weeds" and a "menace to civilization." Her ideology of death and racism was spread worldwide. As recorded on the Life Education and Resource Network's website (see www.blackgenocide.org/planned.html), she said, "Colored people are like human weeds and are to be exterminated." Sanger attempted to use sterilization and contraception as a means to decrease the population of African Americans. Sanger used her affluence to influence, spreading her ideology particularly through newsletters.

Although, as an atheist and an occult practitioner, Sanger had disdain for Christians, she deceptively kept her motives hidden and used black clergy during the early- to mid-1900s to carry and disguise her message, unbeknownst to them. She also got racist white pastors in the South involved in her agenda through their sponsoring of tent revivals. Black congregants were told that before they went into the revival tents, they first must go into Sanger's tent, where they were spoken to about sterilization.

Many pastors were outraged and resisted these efforts. Others, however, were blinded by Sanger's charisma, money and power and were manipulated by her, and thus the plan infiltrated the black community. Sadly, some clergy even went beyond mere toleration and operated in full agreement with her agenda. Through Margaret Sanger, the spirit of Jezebel was able to make her deception work through influence in the Church.

Abortion's Devastation

Though Sanger's motives were not exposed in the past, they since have been revealed through her memoirs. Greg Keath, an African-American leader in the fight to end abortion in America, thoroughly researched her documents in the 1980s. What he found, which is included in Grant's book, was appalling. In a letter to a board member dated December 10, 1939, for example, Sanger wrote the following regarding her project, code-named

"The Negro Project": "We do not want word to go out that we want to exterminate the Negro population and the minister is the man who can straighten out that idea if it ever occurs to any of their more rebellious members."

Grant also writes, "Since minority communities are the primary targets for contraceptive services, Blacks and Hispanics inevitably must bear the brunt of the abortion holocaust." In many communities, abortions among African Americans outstrip births three to one. Our people are truly perishing for lack of knowledge. We have been influenced to believe the lies of the enemy.

Margaret Sanger's philosophy of population control began many organizations, including Planned Parenthood. The statistics regarding abortion in our communities are staggering. As of this writing, 57 million babies have been aborted in America. The effects of abortion on the African-American community have been particularly devastating. We are the only race on the decline in America. The lives of hundreds of thousands of African-American babies are snuffed out every year. Close to 1,500 are aborted every day. Though African Americans account for only 11 percent of the population, more than 35 percent of all babies aborted in America are African American. I hope you caught that—35 percent of all abortions nationwide come from only 11 percent of the population: African Americans!

Why are these statistics so disproportionately high, since there is no doubt in my mind that blacks as a whole do not support the philosophies of this institution of death? Is the fact that 75 percent of all abortion clinics are located in minority communities contributing to this holocaust? Maybe it is because the same spirits of death and racism from Sanger's Jezebelic influence are attacking us today. Margaret Sanger was a mere pawn in the enemy's hands.

"Freakonomics"

Eugenic influence is still pervasive today, even going one step further than Sanger. In the *New York Times* bestseller *Freakonomics* (William Morrow, 2005), authors Steven Levitt and Stephen Dubner report a study claiming that crime rates went down during the wave of crack cocaine use in the 1980s and 1990s—which affected the inner city most greatly—not because of better jobs, better law enforcement or better legislation, but because of abortion. Here is the hypothesis: Unwantedness leads to high crime; legalized abortion leads to less unwantedness; legalized abortion, therefore, leads to less crime. In their words, abortion had an "unintended benefit": reduced crime.

As I was on an airplane, reading *Freakonomics* for the first time, I literally had to catch my breath when I came across the words "unintended benefit." When did killing innocent people become an unintended benefit? The underlying suggestion I discerned from this book, though probably not intended by the authors, is that Satan would love to use this message as an influence to say that African Americans, because of our perceived high level of unwanted babies, which in turn supposedly produces high crime, are better off dead, and America is better off without us. According to this sick influence, abortion in the black community, in essence, is a benefit that reduces murder and other crimes. *What if some hate group got a hold of this?* I thought. Then I said to myself, *Is this subtle enough to influence even decent people, who wouldn't consider themselves to be racists?*

I thought this was absurd, until I turned to the white woman next to me, who was very pleasant and cordial as we talked during our flight and did not appear to be a racist or have any gross biases. When I mentioned to her what I had read in *Freakonomics*, her reply shocked me, and it shocked her, too. Without thinking, she said, "Well, I guess if the abortion rate was higher among African Americans, crime and murder rates would go down." Then she immediately gave me a look that said, "I wish I could take those words back," followed by several "I mean, I mean" statements.

I remembered how a well-known conservative writer and talk show host made a similar slip of the tongue. I do not think folks like these are racists. I do believe, however, that an unspoken suggestion is influencing their response. This same suggestion is influencing the black community, as seen in the dirge of death we call hip hop and gangsta rap music. Gangsta rapper 50 Cent's movie, *Get Rich or Die Tryin'*, shouts to our youth that if they are not rich, they are better off dead.

The impulsive responses by the woman on the plane and others are an indicator that there is an influence, beyond racial implications, that says, "Unintended, unexpected people are better off dead. Let's abort them before they cause society any trouble."

I know a woman named Helen who had an unexpected pregnancy ten years after giving birth to her other children, even though doctors had told her that she could not have any more babies. When she went to check on what she thought was a tumor, she found out she was five months pregnant—with me! I heard another story of a woman who, after being raped, contemplated abortion but changed her mind. Her son is now helping millions of people in Africa and has preached the Gospel around the world. His name is James Robison. A young woman by the name of Mary was scorned for her unexpected, out-of-wedlock pregnancy. Thankfully, she endured the ridicule and gave birth to a little boy, who later died on a cross, rose from the dead and saved the world. His name, of course, is Jesus.

I personally believe the crime rates went down in the '80s and '90s because of another type of "tipping point": when the prayer bowls in heaven released answers to our prayers on earth. After losing so many sons to gang warfare, some praying mothers, I believe, shifted the atmosphere over their neighborhoods. At any rate, statistics can tell us about past trends, but society must be careful when it tries to define anyone's future, void of the involvement of God—who makes the impossible possible. Statistics did not deliver African Americans from slavery. God did! And He wants to deliver us all from the ideologies of abortion, too. In God's economy, children are a blessing from the Lord (see Psalm 127:3).

Part of the reason for African Americans' pain, undoubtedly, is the effects of slavery. The hurts of fatherlessness, which began during this peculiar institution, remain with us. This, of course, does not excuse immoral conduct, but it does shed some light on the fruit we see manifesting today. Satan's remedy has been Planned Parenthood programs and facilities, supposedly established as a means to help and to educate, but instead they have imposed contraceptive alternatives that promote sin and death, showing no hope or future for our children. New technology has uncovered the lies fed to us all. It is not tissue; it is a person.

Remember, influence was believed to be an occult power derived from the stars, and many in ancient Israel were willing to do anything to receive its power, including sacrificing their children. Some sacrificed their children to the star god Molech, likely in an attempt to persuade him to bless their crops (see 2 Kings 23:10; Jeremiah 32:35; Amos 5:26; Zephaniah 1:5; Acts 7:43).

Today we are under the influence of the same god; we just give it a different name: convenience. Whether you call it Jezebel or Molech, it boils down to being the influence of the kingdom of darkness, with its fallen stars that still wage war against the woman and her child (see Revelation 12:4). Anesthetized by Satan's entertainment and amusement, our values have been switched, resulting in our hearts becoming cold and callous.

Demonic, eugenic lies have made us call evil good and good evil. Killing innocent people never has been and never will be a benefit, and no one is unintended or unexpected by God. As a result of our tolerating these lies, our nation has sinned, and the blood of 57 million babies is on our hands. Succumbing to the power of this influence personally cost me years of pain and the life of my first child.

My Story

As I mentioned earlier in this chapter, memories came back to me while I was praying at the Dirksen Building, home of the Senate Judiciary Committee. They were memories of a day many years ago when I walked into an abortion clinic with my girlfriend. This young lady (not my wife) and I were attracted to each other and began a physical relationship. The sad irony is that I had just rededicated my life to Christ. I was growing in my walk with God, but my girlfriend and I fell to temptation and yielded to lust. Before long we were sinning by having premarital sex, and eventually she became pregnant. Afraid of what our parents and others might think of us, we decided to have an abortion. You see, we believed the lie that our child would be better off dead.

My girlfriend was about six weeks pregnant at the time. During this period I was pro-choice. I said to myself, *This is only tissue and not a person yet.* I was wrong. By the time a baby is ten days old, it already has its own DNA, separate from its mother's; three weeks later, it has its own heartbeat; and within six to eight weeks, every organ is in place. Through my own sin and compromise, I did something I will always regret.

One of the things I recalled is how duped I felt that day in the abortion clinic. I remembered realizing how bombarded we are with sexual innuendo by the media. I felt conned by every lustful song I heard on the radio. I felt betrayed by every seductive roadside billboard ad. I felt deceived by every sexually explicit TV show. As I said before, the devil didn't make me do it, but he was by no means an innocent bystander.

The pain of abortion can linger for years, but God is still a healer and redeemer. While I was praying at the Dirksen Building, God revealed another area of pain that needed healing. I had repented in remorse over what I had done. I had forgiven everyone involved twenty years ago, from my girlfriend to the doctor to myself. But God was dealing with an area I had not addressed. For the first time, I felt the pain of missing the opportunity to hold that child in my arms. Somehow over the years I had stuffed this painful emotion, but now God allowed it to come to the surface.

I just wept and kept saying over and over, "I never got to hold my child. God, I miss my baby."

Abortion: Our Fig Leaf

I wish I could say I was not a Christian at the time of this story so many years ago, but I was. As I have shared this story many times, I have found that I am not alone. As it turns out, abortion is the "fig leaf" in the Church: We use it to cover up our sexual immorality.

I have shared my testimony in churches across the country and have prayed for women and men of all races who have been scarred because of this issue. Through women's tears, I have heard stories of how their fathers forced them to have abortions because they wanted church titles of "pastor," "deacon" or "elder" more than the title of "grandfather." I have met women whose mothers wanted to look respectable rather than respect the life of their grandchild. I have even met married but remorseful couples who realized they had sacrificed their child for convenience, in repentant hindsight wishing they had kept their baby and instead sacrificed by getting an extra job. Twenty years ago, I felt the same way.

My experience at the abortion clinic is one I will never forget. While there, I saw other people from my school. People sat, sighing, crying and glancing at each other with blank looks. We all knew why the others were there, and no one said a word. We did not chitchat and smile. We did not make small talk about school. We just glimpsed at each other and then shamefully looked away.

When they called my girlfriend's name, something inside said to me, *Don't do it. This is a child, not a choice.* As I bowed my head, I asked for God's forgiveness. For the first time, I knew and was convicted that

> Abortion is the "fig leaf" in the Church: We use it to cover up our sexual immorality.

this was a person, this was my child. Suddenly, my girlfriend came out. She said to me, "Let's go." Because she was back so quickly, I assumed that she had changed her mind. As we left, I actually felt relieved. Yes, I was afraid of our parents, but I was starting to feel thankful that our child would be born. I asked my girlfriend what happened and if she had changed her mind. She replied, "No, I went through with it. I had the abortion." Our hearts sank.

She said it happened so fast. She told me how the young women were hastily placed in stirrups and the doctor methodically went from room to room performing the procedure. She said it was a very cold environment. Girls were not allowed to grieve or mourn in the clinic. She said that some were stumbling around and crying, so they were not allowed to exit out of the front of the clinic because their crying might change the minds of others. Other girls were rushed out before the grieving settled in.

After my girlfriend described what happened, we sat silently in the car for at least four hours—not saying a word to each other as the remorse began to settle in even more. Given the same set of circumstances and what I know today, I believe we would have made a decision to keep the baby.

We must address this issue in the Church and in our nation. It is time for brokenness, transparency and honesty to come to the Church. We must remove our judgment seats so that people can come to the mercy seat and be healed. By the Lord's grace and mercy, at a prayer meeting in the seat of the Senate Judiciary Committee, God graciously met me and opened heaven. By His mercy, He healed my last bit of pain.

I had to walk into the foyer of the Dirksen Building so that I would not distract others with my loud sobbing. I was soon met by a dear friend who is a spiritual mother to many. She came over to me, and we prayed together. She then asked me, "Will, have you ever asked the Lord to let you know the gender of the child you have in heaven or asked Him to give you a name for your son or daughter? It could bring great healing and closure." I thought, *In all my years of dealing with this abortion, I have never thought of asking God to do this for me.* I said, "No, but let's do it."

As we prayed, I suddenly had a mental picture of my child, and so did my friend. I described what I saw, and she finished the description. We were seeing the same vision. I have a son in heaven! I then asked the Lord the name He wanted me to give my son, and I shared what I heard with her. She heard the same thing from the Lord: I was to bestow honor to my son by naming him after me. I am the proud father of a son in heaven whose name is William Lawrence Ford IV.

The Power of Standing in the Gap

As I share this testimony in churches around the country, sometimes God leads me to do identificational repentance. In other words, I number myself among the transgressors and stand in the gap, representing men who were involved in the pregnancy of women in the audience who had abortions. The Lord showed me that this is often an unresolved issue for women who have had abortions, because no man has ever repented of his involvement.

After leading the men in prayers of repentance, I encourage those who have been responsible for a woman's abortion to come forward and stand with me. I then invite women who have had abortions to stand as the other men and I ask them to forgive us on behalf of the men they shared this experience with. We ask them to forgive us for succumbing to media lies and treating them like sex objects. We ask them to forgive us for abandoning them, for not wanting their children. We ask them to forgive us for not being willing to sacrifice for their babies and not wanting to be the fathers of their children. We ask them to forgive us for believing that our children would be better off dead.

As I have done this, God has been faithful to heal people and bring closure to this wounded area of their hearts. Years of shame, anger, betrayal, resentment, depression and suicide are broken as the presence of God comes into the atmosphere. Lives have been not only healed but saved.

After one powerful Sunday morning service, without any request or prompting, women came forward who were contemplating abortions but had now changed their minds and decided to keep their children! One was a young lady who had scheduled an abortion for the day before, but as God would have it, she overslept and missed the appointment. She then came to church that Sunday, listened to my testimony and heard the prayers of other men and women. That morning she gave her life back to the Lord and decided to keep her child. Two destinies were turned around, and two lives were saved that day!

One individual told me that after hearing me speak, he has prayed for women and men who have been involved in abortions, and has seen God bring not only emotional healing but physical healing as well. One couple, for example, had problems conceiving, but when they repented regarding abortion, the curse of barrenness was broken. They now have their first child!

Some have asked me, "Why address this issue and expose yourself? This could cost you." They feel that if I address this issue in the Church, pretty soon my phone will stop ringing with speaking engagements. Though this is not my only message, it is dear to my heart, and God has been faithful to allow me to share it. You see, I understand the purpose for my favor. I have had incredible favor over my life, and if I remained silent on this issue, I am pretty sure more doors would open. I can use whatever favor I have to serve myself, or I can totally surrender to being a godly influence and be a voice for the voiceless. Who will be a voice for the unborn?

Many people do not want to deal with the reality or the pain of abortion within the Church, but God does. The healing I have seen come to women and men across America, as well as the babies who have been saved, is well worth any sacrifice of my reputation, which is hidden in Christ anyway. I do not want to be a celebrity; I want to be a star and see individuals and families changed by Christ's love.

I believe God wants to raise up a generation who will trade favor for influence and pray in a revival that will heal the pain of abortion. The God who ended slavery is the same God who ended segregation, and He can end abortion, too! If we empty ourselves of our racist baggage, which in many ways influenced abortion in America, God can use Christians of all races to bring justice to the unborn. We must continue until abortion is no longer legal in this nation and a love for life is written on our hearts again.

Changing laws is one thing; changing hearts is another. We are praying not only for laws to change but, more importantly, that the law of God is written on people's hearts. Until laws change, we pray for people to value life and choose not to have abortions. We also pray for the Church to be prepared to help aid and receive people in need. Revival is key to this change of heart. And until then, we keep looking and helping those in need. We establish crisis pregnancy centers and adoption agencies. We touch hurting people with Christ's compassion. We share the Gospel one on one. We share God's love and resources in the workplace. We pray and maintain active involvement as Christ's salt and leaven in society.

God's Irony and Justice

In God's providence and irony, the healing and closure that happened for me at the Senate Judiciary Committee building was on January 17, 2005, or 1/17/05. While in prayer after this encounter, the Lord had me focus on this date and brought to my mind Luke 1:17, which promised that John the Baptist, as the forerunner of the Messiah, would "turn the hearts of the fathers to their children." This is exactly what happened to me. On 1/17 God turned my heart back to my child in heaven, bringing healing and closure.

Luke 1:17 goes on to say that God would use John the Baptist to turn the hearts of "the disobedient to the attitude of the righteous" (NASB). I believe that God was speaking to me about the righteous attitude of the justice generation of Dr. King's era, whose birthday we were celebrating on 1/17. Like Naboth, he and others gave their lives fighting for their inheritance, resisting the powers of their day. Their memory is still influencing us today, beckoning us to be a voice for the voiceless.

Unfortunately, I need to mention that, in reference to my dream, part of the baggage that must be left behind is the mistake civil rights leaders made in succumbing to Jezebel's influence.

Dr. King and others were deceived by Sanger's affluence and charm. Some of those leaders who are alive today, such as Jesse Jackson, have even reversed their stand on abortion from pro-life to pro-choice. Nonetheless, in God's eyes, the rightful heirs of the civil rights movement are the unborn. By connecting to the previous courage of the civil rights leaders, and not their missteps, we can and must advance justice for the unborn.

Even the name of the building that houses the Senate Judiciary Committee is symbolic. It was named after Senator Everett Dirksen, who was instrumental in ending the filibuster that was blocking the civil rights movement. I believe God is calling this generation to pick up the justice mantle of our forefathers, crying out for the civil rights of the unborn. God is calling us to their righteous attitudes, which never wavered, even unto death. His desire is that we raise up a "filibuster of prayer" until a shift comes in America's courts. With the zeal of Jehu, let's not spurn the sacrifice of the previous generation but rather build on what they started.

In that building, I received closure to one of the most painful chapters of my life. My prayer is that from this same building, the prospective new Supreme Court justices and federal court of appeals judges who come before the Senate Judiciary Committee will be used to end this painful chapter in America's history.

EXERCISING INFLUENCE *through Prayer*

Father, the U.S. symbol for justice is blindfolded, but Your justice is not veiled. You see and judge righteously, calling sin what it is—sin. Forgive us of our callous hearts as we ask for a heart of flesh. Release the convicting power of the Holy Spirit, and break our hearts over this issue of blood. Father, forgive us for making a covenant with death and shedding innocent blood through abortion. Forgive us for sacrificing our children to convenience. Forgive us for calling good evil and evil good.

O God, please remove the veil from the eyes of those in the judicial system, and expose the holocaust taking place. Release the wailing women and men who will cry aloud and spare not. O Lord, raise up an outcry, and release the new justice movement that will contend for the civil rights of the unborn.

Turn the hearts of the fathers to the children and the hearts of the children to the fathers once again. O God, break this curse of death from Molech and Jezebel. Turn this disobedient generation back to the attitude of the righteous who fought with Your mantle of justice in their day. Release the spirit of Elijah, and change the atmosphere over the courts so radically until no one agrees with the sick ideology of abortion and euthanasia! Change the atmosphere over the nations so radically until abortion becomes an absurdity and every life is valued!

Jesus, I thank You that Your innocent blood shed on Calvary is superior to the blood on our hands. We cry out, "Have mercy!" Heal men and women who have been traumatized by abortion. God, if mercy triumphs over judgment, then we ask that mercy win again. Have mercy on us, and save us. Spare us from the judgment we have wrought. O God, break and annul our covenant with death so that generations even yet to be created may praise You. In Jesus' name, Amen.

9

The Shepherd's Air Force

ON DECEMBER 11, 2003, I had a powerful dream. In the dream, I was riding with a group of people in an SUV when I looked out the window and saw an eagle sitting on the ground. As we stared at each other, the eagle took off in the direction that we were driving, toward the house in which I lived when I was growing up. Then the eagle disappeared into the western sky—into a thick, bright-white cumulus cloud. Suddenly parts of the cloud began to stream down like columns connecting with the earth. One of these cloud columns began to roll toward me and, surprisingly, delivered to me a large pair of binoculars.

I picked up the binoculars and kept looking as the cloud columns merged together and descended on the western end of the street of my boyhood home. As I was pondering the peculiarity of this cloud, a white light within the cloud began to glow brighter, and then I suddenly saw the silhouette of the Lord standing in the street, surrounded by the cloud. Although very much afraid, I was equally excited, thinking I was about to see Him. Instead, the cloud opened and I saw my wife wearing a nightgown and standing in the street next to the Lord. She extended her hand, gesturing for me to come into the cloud, and said, "What are you waiting for? Come on in." I took her hand and walked through the opening. And then the dream ended. When I awoke, the presence of the Lord was very strong in my room.

In praying for interpretation, I realized there were many significant symbols in this dream. The eagle represented America and the prophetic. The columns coming down from the cloud represented God's government coming to earth ("Thy Kingdom come"). The binoculars represented the seer and watchman anointing being distributed.

I also realized the western direction was significant. The latter rain clouds of Israel come out of the west. "Ask the LORD for rain in the time of the latter rain. The LORD will make flashing clouds; He will give them showers of rain, grass in the field for everyone" (Zechariah 10:1 NKJV). "From the west, men will fear the name of the LORD, and from the rising of the sun, they will revere his glory. For he will come like a pent-up flood that the breath of the LORD drives along" (Isaiah 59:19).

My wife was symbolic of Christ's Bride, the Church. Her being dressed in a nightgown highlighted the context of nighttime and represented readiness through prayer—night and day, 24 hours a day, 7 days a week. Her beckoning me to come into the cloud with her and the Lord represented the Scripture that says, "The Spirit and the bride say, 'Come!'" (Revelation 22:17). The house that the Lord was visiting in my dream represented a group of believers or a movement bound together in prayer— what many of us call a "house of prayer"—but more specifically, because of the columns and the eagle, it represented governmental houses of prayer in America.

My dream reminded me of Daniel 7:

> I kept looking in the night visions, and behold, with the clouds of heaven One like a Son of Man was coming. . . . I kept looking, and that horn was waging war with the saints and overpowering them until the Ancient of Days came and judgment was passed in favor of the saints of the Highest One, and the time arrived when the saints took possession of the kingdom.
>
> Daniel 7:13, 21–22 NASB

Just as Daniel kept looking for God's justice from His heavenly court, I knew I was given binoculars in this dream to keep looking until favor comes in the form of justice in the courts of America. God is calling many of us to governmental intercession.

God's Dream House

I recorded my dream and sent it to others for their consideration. Less than a month after having the dream, I received an incredible confirmation. While ministering at the Minnesota Prophetic Conference, I was invited by a local pastor to speak at his church's Sunday service. After the conference, I left with him and his wife to stay at their house. As he drove, the Lord brought back to my mind the dream, with the eagle, the binoculars and the western cloud, about being a steward of the governmental house of prayer. I suddenly realized we were driving west, which reminded me again of the significance of the western direction in my dream. I did not make too much of this—until we drove westward into St. Cloud, Minnesota! From there we drove into the small town just outside of St. Cloud where the pastor lives: Grey Eagle! Now I had both the western cloud and the eagle from my dream.

As we arrived at the house, he said to me that his house used to be an old abandoned church, built in 1916. He and his wife bought the church and converted the basement into living quarters, because the Lord told them to buy it as a prophetic sign that He was calling them to be stewards of His house. This pastor had no idea that God had been talking to me about stewarding His house of prayer.

When we walked into the living area, hanging on the wall was a set of binoculars, which looked like the ones I had seen in my dream. I asked what they were for, and he said, "Oh, there's an American bald eagles' nest just around the corner, and I love to see them fly around."

What were the chances of having a bald eagles' nest close to one's home? Mind you, I was invited to speak at his church before he heard my dream. Curious about my bewilderment and excitement, he asked what was going on.

I replied, "I think I have a word for your church." That was an understatement! When I shared my dream and all these confirmations, he was blown away. What a setup! Needless to say, we had a powerful and exciting time of ministry at his church. He said to me, "Will, this was the confirmation but not the fulfillment." He was right.

The Governmental House of Prayer

Two days later, I received a business call from the government. My Bible had opened that day to Proverbs 16:15, which says, "In the light of the king's face is life, and his favor is like a cloud of the latter rain" (NKJV). I thought, *That's part of what I saw in my dream, the bright, shining face of the Lord in the western latter rain cloud.* I received a call that the company I owned was being considered for a management project, without our pursuing this project at all, at Sheppard Air Force Base, which is just to the west of us. Because we had favor, the contract to manage and staff the base's 24-hour call center was awarded to us.

It dawned on me one day that the spiritual 24-hour call center should be the house of prayer, which calls upon the name of the Lord. I began to realize that the governmental house of prayer is the *Shepherd's* Air Force. I believe God is calling for young and old eagles to gain air supremacy through intercession and govern earthly matters from the heavens through His 24/7 house of prayer. The Lord is giving us a new pair of binoculars to recognize what He is doing until His appearing. He wants us to watch over the affairs of the nation, seeing the enemy's plans afar off. This excites me! The Shepherd has an Air Force: the governmental house of prayer, God's governmental headquarters on earth.

In this chapter, we will talk about governmental intercession and the need for those in the house of prayer to be engaged in every realm of influence in society. We will focus on the judicial system, particularly the Supreme Court. You will understand our need for focused intercession there and see the results the praying Church is realizing from targeted corporate intercession for our courts. First, let's talk about the need for sustained prayer in our communities and how God uses it to shift the prevailing cultural influence over regions and nations.

The governmental center of the Kingdom of God is the prayer room, or the house of prayer. King David had this understanding and set up a tent for the Ark of the Covenant (see 2 Samuel 6:17), which contained the glory of God. And in this "tabernacle of David" was a 24-hour supply of worship from skilled musicians, priests and Levites (see 1 Chronicles 6:31–49). The fire was never to go out on the altar. Unlike the Tabernacle of Moses or the Temple of Solomon, David's tent, or tabernacle, of prayer God said He would rebuild again in the earth (see Amos 9:11; Acts 15:16–18). And He is doing so through you and me. As a matter of fact, according to 1 Corinthians 6:19, we are now the "temple of the Holy Spirit," where the Spirit of God dwells. Is that not awesome?

The rebuilding of David's tabernacle is not restricted to our personal identity and relationship with God, however. God is establishing 24-hour worship and intercession in the earth, and through it He is releasing His Kingdom influence. Through the governmental headquarters of His Kingdom, the prayer room, God will shift the influence over cultures and nations in a way that will last for generations.

The House of Ill Repute v. the House of Prayer

As we have seen in previous chapters, sustained influence from the kingdom of darkness can create warped ideologies. In fact, the sustained influence and logic over a region often seems absurd to people outside of that culture. Here is one example: Benjamin "Bugsy" Siegel, a mobster and gambler, built the world's largest hotel casino in his day, The Flamingo, in 1947. This hotel was built in the middle of nowhere, in the desert, but Siegel was convinced that people would eventually come from around the world to his hotel in Las Vegas, Nevada. And they did. Today Las Vegas is the gambling Mecca of the world. The spiritual influence there is so powerful that it attracts people from all over the world to gamble away their hard-earned money, even though the odds of winning are against them.

In order to lessen the hurt of losing money, the culture of Las Vegas has developed a strange system of logic. To deaden the pain of blowing their money, visitors typically set aside a cushion of money, sometimes thousands of dollars, that they will not feel bad about losing. Do you see how strange that logic is? People set aside a couple of thousand dollars, just to throw it away in Las Vegas! Think of the good that hard-earned money could do. Clear-thinking people outside of the influence of the culture find this logic absurd—and it is!

As a good example, on the other hand, I have learned about Count Ludwig von Zinzendorf and the Moravians. Led by Zinzendorf, the Moravians began a Christian community that resulted in a 100-year-long prayer meeting. From 1727 to 1827 this prayer meeting never ended. Their motto was "The fire never goes out on the altar." Their other maxim was "One at home, one in the field." As some stayed at the altar of prayer, others went out as missionaries. John and Charles Wesley were converted through their contact with Moravian missionaries. The Moravians began the first Protestant missionary movement. The influence of this Kingdom culture was so powerful that it birthed the First Great Awakening, which transformed the hearts of people in Britain and America and ended slavery. The belief system within the environment was so influential that some of these saints actually sold themselves into slavery in order to preach the Gospel around the world. Now, that sounds absurd to people outside of the Moravians' Kingdom culture, but not to people who are under the influence of Christ's love.

Isn't it interesting that both Bugsy Siegel and Ludwig von Zinzendorf sustained spiritual influence that has lasted for generations—one from the kingdom of darkness and the other from the Kingdom of light? The sad reality is that such a worldly influence has come into the Church today that some "saints" would rather lose their money in Las Vegas than lose their lives for Jesus Christ. As we have seen with the Moravians, we must dare to believe that sustained worship and prayer, in the spirit of the tabernacle of David, can affect culture and governments again.

God's Ruling Body on Earth

The house of prayer was fueled by the Levites, a special tribe within the people of Israel. From the book of Joshua, we understand that the Levites' inheritance was the offerings made by fire to the Lord and the Lord God Himself (see Joshua 13:14, 33). Their inheritance was a fiery, passionate affection for the living God, and because God was their portion, they could not be bought or sold. We also see how later Levites served in the house of prayer commissioned by David. Not only were they skilled musicians, singers and priests, but they were also called to release God's influence in society. Of the 38,000 Levites mentioned in 1 Chronicles 23:3–5, 24,000 were to supervise the work of the Temple that Solomon would build, 6,000 were to be officials and judges, 4,000 were to be gatekeepers and 4,000 were to be part of the 24-hour prayer and worship team.

In other words, these intercessors took the anointing and the weight of God's glory out of the house of prayer and into society as well. Why would God have a Levite be a judge? Because of his sold-out, fiery devotion to God, he could not be bribed. Levites could not be bought or sold, because they were already sold-out to God. Their decision-making was based not on staying in office but rather on staying in relationship with the Lord. God—not their jobs, titles or offices—was their portion.

We need intercessors in the house of prayer and in every sphere of influence in society today as well. We need "one at home and one in the field." We need people who cannot be bought or sold to be statesmen locally and nationally—people who will extend their prayer meeting into places of authority in society. When the righteous rule, the people are glad, and the culture is shaped by their godly influence.

The word *church* does not mean today what it meant to Jesus' first followers. In our vocabulary, the word has been relegated to describing a Christian-owned building with tax-exempt status. But when Jesus and the apostles used the word *church*, they were talking about the members of Christ's ruling governmental body. Our English word *church* comes from the Greek word *ekklesia*, which literally means "called-out ones" (therefore, "an assembly")—those who were called out to rule in society. In Greece the *ekklesia* described those who were part of the Greek parliament and legislature. In Rome the *ekklesia* were part of the ruling body sent into newly conquered territories. Their job was to make that territory's culture to be like the culture of Rome. Understanding how the word *ekklesia* was used in Jesus' time helps us better appreciate what the New Testament means and value our mandate as Christ's ruling governmental body.

From this we see that we are, as the Church, God's "called-out ones"; we are in the world but not of the world. First, we are to legislate from the heavenly realms with Him in prayer. Then once we have obtained breakthrough in the spirit realm over regions and nations, we are called to advance His Kingdom by sharing the Gospel until the conquered territory on earth reflects the culture of the Kingdom of heaven. Richard Rohr, as quoted in *Engaging the Powers* by Walter Wink (Fortress, 1992), says:

> To pray is to build your house. To pray is to discover that Some-one else is within your house. To pray is to recognize that it is not your house at all. To keep praying is to have no house to protect because there is only One House. And that One House is everybody's Home. . . . That is the politics of prayer. And that probably is why truly spiritual people are always a threat to politicians of any sort. They want our allegiance and we can no longer give it. Our house is too big.

We see this in Acts 12. The evil King Herod was revered by many as a god. He had a following of Jews known as Herodi-ans. When Jesus warned about the Pharisees and the Sadducees, He warned His disciples to beware of the leaven or influence of Herod (see Mark 8:15)—likely a worldly, political spirit. In Acts 12:1–2, we read that Herod killed the apostle James, much to the delight of the Jews who despised the followers of Jesus.

When Herod saw that his "approval ratings" had gone up, he then seized the apostle Peter in order to kill him.

This crisis mobilized the Church to intercession like never before. They held a prayer meeting in the city, contending in prayer until breakthrough came for Peter. Things shifted in the heavens so powerfully through prayer that God sent an angel to free Peter, and the enormous city gates were opened by the angel as Peter was led out of the city. The government of God released justice in this matter, and Peter was set free because of the prayers of the saints.

Not only that, but the influence shifted so drastically in the heavens that Herod came under the dominion of the government of God. While people were cheering as Herod spoke, shouting, "This is the voice of a god, not of a man," because Herod did not give glory to God, he was smitten by an angel, was eaten up with worms and died before all to see (Acts 12:21–23). The amazing thing is that this was more than likely not the first time the people shouted, "This is the voice of a god, not of a man" to Herod. What was the difference this time? The sustained intercession and prayers of the Church. The atmosphere over the entire region had changed; the governance of the heavenly Kingdom exercised its influence on earth, in part because of sustained prayer and intercession.

JHOP

In cities like Atlanta and Kansas City, Missouri, houses of prayer are doing just that. Since 2000, these worship warriors have been praying with live musicians, singers and intercessors 24 hours a day, 7 days a week, 365 days a year. Fueled primarily by passionate young people, and sustained by a focus on intimacy with Christ, this movement has built faith in others to do the same thing across the world. Another place where this is happening is the Justice House of Prayer (JHOP) in Washington, D.C., founded by Lou Engle and led by Matt Lockett, with which I have been more closely affiliated.

JHOP was birthed out of fifty continuous days of prayer, worship and fasting in Colorado Springs, Colorado. During that time, one of our dear friends who was on his way to join us was literally chased down Interstate 70 by a huge tornado. Fortunately, he was unharmed. Two weeks later, however, he saw not just one but two tornadoes—although this time, thankfully, it was in a dream.

In the dream, a group of us were being chased by two tornadoes, but the peculiar thing was that both tornadoes had the letters H and A in them. Chris knew we had to confront the tornadoes that were mocking us, but we could not do so until we first went to the laundromat and washed our clothes. After washing our clothes, we then went to rebuke the tornadoes, and the dream ended.

My friend discerned that the interpretation of the dream is that homosexuality and abortion are the H and A in the tornadoes, which represent a whirlwind of destruction that is mocking the Church (ha-ha) and will destroy our nation if not resisted and addressed. These things can be addressed, however, only after we have been cleansed. Knowing what God was requiring of us, we humbled ourselves as a group, asking for forgiveness and cleansing regarding sexual impurity of all kinds and seeking God's cleansing of all unrighteousness.

The period of time after that included some of the most powerful and strategic prayers of my life. We saw many answers to prayer for our nation. As the fifty days were coming to a close, we began to pray about the next assignment from the Lord, and during that time, God began to speak to Lou about establishing a house of prayer in Washington, D.C. We also felt the leading of the Lord to go across the country rallying intercessors to pray for the next election, which was critical regarding the courts, abortion and same-sex marriage.

While in prayer, we remembered our friend being literally chased down I-70 by a tornado and his *ha-ha* dream. We then looked at Psalm 70 to see if there was any prophetic connection to I-70. We were astonished. Psalm 70:2–4 says, "May those who seek my life be put to shame and confusion; may all who desire my ruin be turned back in disgrace. May those who say to me, 'Aha! Aha!' turn back because of their shame. But may all who seek you rejoice and be glad in you."

Seeing the connection to the *ha-ha* dream, we were astounded. And then we looked at a map and were surprised to see that I-70 goes from Cove Fort in central Utah to near Washington, D.C., creating a dividing line in America. It was as if God was saying to us, "I'm establishing a plumb line of righteousness in America." God was granting an invitation to pray along I-70 as a "highway of holiness," all the way to the nation's capital.

Changing the Influence over Leaders

Remember that one of the English words translated "influence" in the Bible is from the Hebrew root word *yad*, which literally means "hand." This makes sense, because people who are under the influence of something or someone are gradually gripped, subtly becoming captivated by and succumbing to foreign control. Recall how *yad* conveys how influence, like an unseen hand, not only grips but also fashions, shapes and exercises control by turning a person or situation.

The key Scripture where we see this is Proverbs 21:1: "The king's heart is in the hand of the LORD; he directs it like a watercourse wherever he pleases." The word *hand* here is the Hebrew word *yad*, so this verse could read, "The king's heart is *under the influence* of the LORD; he directs it like a watercourse wherever he pleases." I am convinced, however, that the hand of God will not turn a king unless an intercessor grips God's heart in prayer.

An excellent illustration of this is Nehemiah. As cupbearer for the king, Nehemiah had one of the most trusted positions in all of the Persian empire. Nevertheless, he put his coveted position at risk when he found out about the condition of Jerusalem and his fellow Jews who had returned to live there. Brokenhearted, he cried out to God for favor with the king.

When Nehemiah went before King Artaxerxes with a sad countenance, he put his life in jeopardy. No one could come into the presence of the king in those days with a sad countenance. This is why Nehemiah 2:2 says that he was afraid. Yet, in the face of political opposition, fear and death, Nehemiah chose to reflect the broken heart of the King of heaven, and as a result of his prayer and intercession, God gave him influence. The heart of the king was turned by the hand of God to give Nehemiah a leave of absence, along with a military escort and other provisions. Nehemiah testified, "Because the gracious hand [*yad*] of my God was upon me, the king granted my requests" (Nehemiah 2:8). As you can see, because Nehemiah gripped God's heart in prayer, God released His influence (*yad*), which turned the heart of the king. Powerful!

We can see how important it is to pray for those in authority, whether they are kings, presidents, governors, mayors, legislators or councilmen or councilwomen. As a matter of fact, in 1 Timothy 2:1–4 we are *commanded* to pray for them:

> I urge, then, first of all, that requests, prayers, intercession and thanksgiving be made for everyone—for kings and all those in authority, that we may live peaceful and quiet lives in all godliness and holiness. This is good, and pleases God our Savior, who wants all men to be saved and to come to a knowledge of the truth.

The word *first* in the passage is the Greek word *proton*, which means "first in time, place, order and importance." Of utmost importance, our first priority is to pray and give thanks for persons in positions of authority. We do not have to vote for them, but we are commanded to pray for them.

The apostle Paul instructed the saints to pray, intercede and give thanks for their rulers during the reign of one of the most wicked rulers ever, the Roman emperor Nero. The situation is not, therefore, that we should pray for a person in leadership if he or she is a Christian. No, we pray because we are commanded to by the Word of God, because prayer makes a difference. In fact, prayer for governmental leaders is tied to the salvation of people's souls. It is one of the most powerful weapons of evangelism.

> Prayer for governmental leaders is tied to the salvation of people's souls. It is one of the most powerful weapons of evangelism.

If we look at the rulers God used during the Babylonian captivity of Israel—Nebuchadnezzar, Cyrus, Artaxerxes—none of them was a follower of Jehovah, yet God used them because of the prayers and intercession of the saints. All authority to govern society is given by God (see Romans 13:1). Though God grants offices of authority, the people who fill these positions are not always under His influence. Thus, the Church must pray for these rulers' salvation, for God's leadership in their lives, that ungodly counsel will be thwarted and that decisions will be made that will have a positive, righteous influence upon society.

The enemy tries to grip the hearts of these leaders in order to release his influence to enact unrighteous decrees. Psalm 94:20–21 says, "Shall the throne of iniquity, which devises evil by law, have fellowship with You? They gather together against the life of the righteous, and condemn innocent blood" (NKJV). Through the influence of the kingdom of darkness, the devil has set up "thrones of iniquity" in order to legislate demonic decrees that have a profound influence upon society, because laws shape the behavior and conduct of people.

The word for "iniquity" in Psalm 94:20 could also be translated "perversion." The enemy has set up, through our court system, thrones that have legislated the killing of innocent life through abortion and have legislated perversion and sin through same-sex marriage. The establishment of unrighteous laws fortifies and legitimizes sinful behavior, which reinforces the strongholds in people's lives, thus making it harder for them to receive the Gospel.

Our allegiance is not to conservatives or liberals; our allegiance is to the Kingdom of God. As I have heard it said, "Who cares about the left wing or the right wing when the whole bird is sick? We need the Dove [Holy Spirit] back in America!" In other words, we want the government of God to maintain its influence in society, ultimately so that people can hear and receive the Word of God and obtain salvation. Changes can be made through voting, but they will be sustained only through prayer and intercession—which brings about salvation and transforms hearts. The praying Church must now arise and intercede in order that a generation may be saved. Not only is the eternal salvation of people at stake, but so is the offspring of an entire nation.

Shifting the Courts: Prevailing for Life

A caravan of about fifty people drove along Interstate 70 to pray for spiritual breakthroughs and for God's influence in the 2004 elections. During a stop in Washington, D.C., God moved on the hearts of several businessmen and leaders to help fund the

Justice House of Prayer. In a building shaped like an arrowhead, which points toward the Supreme Court, prayer and intercession are made daily to see abortion in America and the humanistic influence over the court turned around. Young people are praying not only at the JHOP building but also, based upon a dream, in front of the steps of the Supreme Court.

Praying for L-I-F-E

One JHOP leader had a dream in which he saw another person and me leading thousands of people to the steps of the Supreme Court to pray. In this dream, my prayer partner's oldest son was also present. He had duct tape over his mouth and L-I-F-E written on the tape. We were praying in agreement with the unheard prayers of babies being aborted in America. We received this dream as a strategic prayer assignment from the Lord and have been interceding this way ever since.

As I was praying in front of the Supreme Court in this manner, my Bible opened to Exodus 14:14: "The LORD will fight for you while you keep silent" (NASB). What an encouragement to my heart that God was hearing our prayers and fighting on behalf of the voiceless!

People have come up to us and asked if we are protesting, and our simple reply is, "No, we're just appealing to a greater and higher Court." We could pray in private, and we do not want to be thought of as Pharisees who are parading their deeds around for everyone to see. On the contrary, we feel we are humbling ourselves by carrying out a mandate. Our assignment is to pray onsite with insight until the manifold wisdom of God changes the dark, demonic influence of principalities and powers over the Supreme Court. We believe that sustained intercession is changing what we cannot see in the unseen realm (see Ephesians 3:10).

Is it paying off? Only history will tell, as important decisions come before the court. But during this season of intercession, we were given dreams and prayer strategies regarding seats on the Supreme Court that could be filled through the influence of the praying Church. Like Daniel appealing to the court of heaven in Daniel 7, we "kept looking."

The Court above the Courts

The Lord began to speak to me about the Supreme Court through dreams in 2005. The first dream came to me when I was feeling defeated about the court's decision on February 22 not to hear *Roe v. Wade*. This decision was by no means a final blow to ending abortion; other cases are coming before the court, and this fight will not end overnight. Nonetheless, that night I felt crushed, and I cried myself to sleep. But God brought me encouragement through a "basketball court" dream.

I was playing basketball against the Supreme Court justices in the dream, and babies and toddlers were my teammates. The justices, wearing their black robes, were scoring repeatedly and wearing us out. I felt weak and lethargic in the dream. But then I suddenly remembered who I was, that I had played basketball in college, and I began to exert myself on the court. Justice David Souter tried to shoot a jump shot on the left side of the court, and I blocked his shot. Justice Sandra Day O'Connor retrieved the ball, but as she was dribbling, I stole the ball from her, went to the other end of the court and made a layup. The momentum began to shift in the game, and the dream ended.

When I awoke, the Lord told me that the basketball court represented the highest court in the land, the Supreme Court, and the judicial system of America. He assured me that, while it may not seem like it, we are gaining strength in our fight for the babies. We must remember who we are and the power we have in fervent, effectual prayer. He said we must stay in the court battle for abortion to end in America. God was saying to me, "The momentum is shifting, and they don't have the last shot!"

Needless to say, I was encouraged and prayed over this dream continually. Months later Sandra Day O'Connor surprised everyone and decided to step down! I remembered dreaming about her. While I was in prayer, the Lord said to me, "I'm taking the ball of abortion out of her hands, and if the Church will pray, I will raise up a justice who will block the shots [of those who promote it]."

Who Is John Roberts?

Shortly after I had this dream, one of the JHOP interns had a brief but profound dream. In her dream, she was approached by a man who said to her that John Roberts would be the next Supreme Court justice. "Who is John Roberts?" we asked. This dream was given to her several weeks before any list of hopefuls was published by the White House. When the list was later published, we were astonished to learn that a man named John Roberts was on it. After learning about him through research, we began praying that God would appoint him because of his past views against abortion.

Many in Washington were unaware of John Roberts, because most people, including President George W. Bush's aides, were saying that Judge Edith Brown Clement was going to receive the nomination. Not sure of who she was but believing that God had given this dream for a reason, JHOP became more convinced to pray for John Roberts. Other leaders and I joined these young people in prayer, even flying to Washington in order to pray with them. We were told that, to the surprise of his aides, just hours before his announcement, the President turned to his aides and said he was choosing John Roberts. The Church gripped God's heart in prayer and President Bush came under the influence of God's hand (*yad*) from heaven, which turned him like a watercourse in the direction the Lord wanted the President to go (see Proverbs 21:1).

The New Jersey

The next nominee was Harriet Miers. Neither I nor anyone else felt anything right or wrong about her, but after we sought the Lord in prayer, another intercessor was given a dream. In the dream, he was watching Ms. Miers approach an open seat on the Supreme Court, but she could not sit there, because the chair had been reserved, with a new green basketball jersey, for the next member of the court. The day after he had this dream, Harriet Miers, to our surprise, withdrew from the nomination process.

JHOP began praying in light of this dream, and within a few weeks, the nomination of Samuel Alito emerged. He just happens to be from New Jersey, which is nicknamed the Garden State. This would explain the "new jersey" that was green, like a garden, in the dream. After hearing about Alito's past views against abortion, we began to sense that this seat was reserved for him and that we must pray against any filibuster by raising up a filibuster of prayer. Though the vote was close, Judge Alito was confirmed without a filibuster.

Just before Alito's confirmation hearing, the basketball court theme surfaced again. On November 28, 2005, several news outlets reported that a "basketball-sized piece of marble" (the reporters' words, not mine) fell from the facade over the entrance to the Supreme Court building. I could not help thinking about the consistent siege of prayers that is shifting the atmosphere over the Supreme Court and all the basketball court dreams that I and others have had related to the Supreme Court.

Full-Court Press

It just so happened that Lou Engle and JHOP were being interviewed by ABC's *Nightline* the day this happened. One intercessor told me that the basketball-sized piece of marble fell down as she walked up to pray at the Supreme Court that day. She also said that reporters who came to report the story even held up basketballs in order to show viewers how large the piece of marble was that fell. Architects had recently checked the building, and they said they were baffled as to why this particular piece of marble broke off and fell from the structure.

I believe this entire event is prophetic: from the piece of marble falling from the facade (representing "masks" coming off the court by shaking), to its authority figures coming down (God breaking the false ideologies that are influencing perverted justice), to its breaking into forty pieces (representing a generational breakthrough of forty years).

Another point of interest is that the Supreme Court actually has a basketball court just above its chambers. There is even a light in this gym that comes on to let people know when the court below is in session. This basketball court's nickname is "the highest court in the land." So yes, there is a "court" above the Supreme Court. But furthermore, this physical reality is an awesome reminder of the spiritual reality that the highest court in the land is the Supreme Court of heaven—where the Judge of the universe and His advocate Son rule in the midst of all enemies. Our job in intercession is to pray until the will of God is done on earth as it is in heaven, until "justice roll[s] down like waters and righteousness like an ever-flowing stream" (Amos 5:24 NASB).

While in prayer, I was reminded of the piece of marble that fell from the Supreme Court building and of the fact that basketball players sometimes refer to a basketball as "the rock." At crucial times in a basketball game, key players take ownership of the opportunity at hand. In those moments, they do not say, "Pass the basketball, please." No, they demand the ball, saying, "Give me the rock!" I believe this is our cry, too, but we are calling for God. The Rock of our salvation, the Stone that was rejected, is taking His place in our courts.

Isaiah 33:22, which this nation's government was founded upon, says, "The LORD is our judge, the LORD is our lawgiver, the LORD is our king; it is he who will save us." God is calling our country to look to Christ, the Rock from which this nation was hewn. In humility we must fall on the Rock and be broken over our condition, or the Rock will fall on us in crushing humiliation (see Matthew 21:42–44). This generation cannot pass this issue on to the next generation; we must address it now. Because of all the prayers in the court battle for the next generation and because of our united cry of "Give us the Rock!"—God, the Rock of Ages, will answer with Himself.

I believe that now is the time for another "full-court press" on the judicial system. We must provoke people to pray as never before for justice for the unborn. Listen: The court does not have the last shot; the praying Church does. I love what my Christian brother Jay Comiskey says about this: "The old is falling down before His authority as we 'strike the scales of justice' in prayer. Perhaps this is a small token and sign of what is transpiring in the spirit realm. The authority of Christ Jesus is rising over the Supreme Court. Everything will crash and fall in His presence!"

Let's Ask God for the Rock

It is time to humble ourselves and appeal to the court of heaven, which is above every other court. I believe that the momentum is shifting. The time has come to strike the scales of justice again in prayer.

The piece of stone that fell from the Supreme Court building broke into forty pieces, which could represent the ending of a wilderness period in the courts. Just as important, we have received dreams revealing that if the Church does not pray, then those we have prayed onto the court will succumb to the prevailing humanistic influence over it, as other justices have done in the past. We must be thermostats and prevail in prayer until the influence is shifted over the Supreme Court. Like Daniel, let's attentively keep looking in prayer until the Ancient of Days passes judgment on behalf of the saints of the Highest One. Through prayer, let's put it in the hands of the Lord.

Let's ask God for the Rock!

Remember, we are praying not only for laws to change but more importantly that the law of God be written in people's hearts. Until laws change, we pray for people to value life, always looking through the binoculars of hope. Revival is key to this change of heart, but in the meantime, we keep looking and practically helping those in need. We keep looking and establish crisis pregnancy centers and touch hurting people with Christ's compassion. We keep looking and share the Gospel one on one. We keep looking, through prayer and active involvement as Christ's leaven in society. We keep looking until there is no end to His influence and peace (see Isaiah 9:7).

> It is time to dream again! God wants us to pick up His binoculars and soar with Him in prayer.

You have probably noticed that almost every testimony in this book is connected to a dream. As I prayed about writing this book, I felt the leading of the Lord in this direction. I believe God desired this because He wants us to believe that, even against all hope, dreams still come true. This refers not only to visions in the night but also to aspirations. Many have been influenced by the enemy to give up on America, but God has not. As my dear friend Paul Cole says, "We must recover the ability to dream that the world can be a better place."

I believe God still has a dream for your nation—and you are in it. Beloved, it is time to dream again! God wants us to pick up His binoculars and soar with Him in prayer. Together let's keep looking until there is no end to Christ's influence and increase in our life and nation (see Isaiah 9:7).

EXERCISING INFLUENCE *through Prayer*

God, as we peer through binoculars of wisdom and revelation, we see that in America there is a court above the Supreme Court—the Supreme Court of heaven. Like Daniel, we keep looking until the Ancient of Days releases justice in our courts again. We thank You, Father, for the blood of Your advocate Son, Jesus, and we offer it as our plea for every judge and for our judicial system. Lord, we say that man does not have the last word over homosexuality, abortion or our nation's destiny—but You do. The enemy mockingly laughs (ha-ha), but, God, You will not be mocked.

We proclaim that the whirlwind of destruction that is coming because of sin will be averted, because You are cleansing us. We thank You that You are laughing at the enemy from Your heavenly throne and saying, "Why do the people rage and plot a vain thing?" You get the last laugh, Jesus. We thank You that the momentum is shifting in the hearts of people. We thank You for striking the scales of justice, but, Lord, please do not stop until this nation— and every nation—is completely turned in Your direction.

We peer through our binoculars and see a cloud the size of a man's hand coming on the horizon. If the hearts of kings are under the influence of Your hand, O Lord, raise up the house of prayer that will contend with every other house in the nations. May the influence in the house of prayer shift the prevailing influence over the leaders of nations. God, save their souls and grip them by Your hand. And God, thwart the counsel of every "Ahithophel," in the name of Jesus.

Shut the door to the evil one's influence on our leaders. Let only those who are blameless minister to them. May the Church get out of its four walls and be Your ruling governmental body (ekklesia) in every sphere of society, removing thrones of iniquity. We proclaim, in Jesus' name, that the gates of hell will not prevail against us.

We keep looking, and we see that salvation is coming to every ghetto, every suburb, every tribe and every tongue. We keep looking and see the death culture ending in America, with every life being valued in this nation. We keep looking and see the Sun of Righteousness coming with healing in His wings for the nations of the earth. We keep looking and say, "Kingdom of God, come! Will of God, be done!" We agree with the Spirit and the Bride, who say, "Come!" In Jesus' name, Amen.

10

Jesus and the Marketplace

LANDA COPE IS FOUNDING INTERNATIONAL DEAN of the College of Communication for Youth With A Mission's University of the Nations. She writes of the time she came upon a television program that told of a British journalist who put to the test the Christian notion that the greater the Christian presence, the greater the benefit to society. Through a series of studies conducted in the 1990s on major cities in America, this journalist and his research team eventually found the city with most church-going Christians, in relation to the population of the city. They then looked at the social demographics of that city. These variables included crime rate, health care, education, jobs and homelessness.

After studying these variables and others, they found that the city with the most Christians per capita, shockingly, was also one of the least desirable cities to live in at that time. That city was Dallas, Texas. In response, Landa Cope writes,

By the time my English host was done with the Dallas study I was devastated. No one would want to live in a city in that condition. The crime, the decrepit social systems, the disease, the economic discrepancies, the racial injustice all disqualified this community from having an adequate quality of life. And this was the "most Christianized" city in America. I wanted to weep.

The program was not finished. The host took this devastating picture of a broken community to the Christian leaders and asked for their observations. He chose leaders of status and integrity. He chose the kind of Christian leaders other Christians would respect. One by one, each pastor viewed the same facts that I had just seen about the condition of his city. With simplicity, the narrator asked each minister, "As a Christian leader, what is your response to the condition of your community?" Without exception, in various ways, they all said the same thing, "This is not my concern. . . . I'm a spiritual leader."

In other words, these leaders, like many others, focused on making sure these people had "fire insurance" per Mark 16:15, but were not carrying out our Matthew 28:19 mandate to make disciples, which is what affects the culture. After a time of seeking the Lord for answers, Cope concluded that the problem is this: Christians have focused on preaching the Gospel of salvation, not the Gospel of the Kingdom, which encompasses both salvation and discipleship for applying biblical principles in every facet of life. (See more from The Template Institute online at http://templateinstitute.com/the-old-testament-template-book-chapter-1/#sthash.Do7R1JUQ.dpuf.)

Dallas, Texas—the city featured in this study as the place with the greatest percentage of Christians, yet the least desirable living conditions—is my hometown! Upon reading Cope's story, my heart sank. I, too, was devastated by the reality that in the city in which I do life, arguably, the epicenter of the American "Bible belt," researchers found little-to-no evidence of Christians having any impact on the culture in the late '90s.

That period was rough in the Dallas/Fort Worth metroplex, and Dallas in particular. The city council was divisive; the school board was riddled with scandals; shoddy treatment of the homeless was making national news; and crime and murder in Dallas were among the highest in the nation. Though there has been some improvement over the years, the Church has left a minor imprint upon the very city in which mega-ministries and massive church buildings abound. The same can be said for other cities, of course, and it is time for us to take responsibility for their condition!

In this chapter, we will discuss the importance of being actively engaged in the marketplace to influence society at large. We will also take a look at the difference between countercultures and subcultures, and how they are used to shift the mainstream culture. Lastly, we will look at examples of Kingdom entrepreneurs effectively influencing the marketplace and bringing about positive change in society.

The *Ekklesia*—Discipling Nations

You may recall from a previous chapter that the word *ekklesia* means "church." It is interesting to note where Jesus was when He introduced this concept for the first time. Jesus was looking upon the city of Caesarea Philippi, a city ruled by an ungodly council and built upon a rock of demonic idolatry and worship of Zeus, Pan and Caesar. Jesus chose this site to proclaim that upon the Rock of the truth—the truth that He is the Christ, the Son of the Living God—He will build His church or *ekklesia*.

Beyond a mere assembly or building, He was referring to His ruling governmental Body, the council of the "called-out" ones, which is the better definition of *ekklesia*. He also confronted the demonic influence, stating that the gates of hell would not prevail against His *ekklesia*! He said further that in the face of the spiritual powers at Caesarea Philippi, He would give His *ekklesia* the keys to the Kingdom of heaven, to bind and loose things in heaven and on earth. Powerful!

Please understand: People at that time never would have thought Jesus was referring to a building or assembly of people, as we understand *ekklesia* or *church* today. In Greek and Roman society, *ekklesia* referred to a ruling government, a body of people called out of society that met several times a year. The *ekklesia* chose judges, made laws and decrees, declared war and strategized. In order to convene a meeting of the *ekklesia*, six thousand people had to be present. Otherwise, their decrees were not legal or binding. The Roman empire sent out its *ekklesia* into newly conquered territory in order to prepare that area for Rome's rulership. The *ekklesia* erected artwork, taught in the schools, brought in music and literature, all to disciple and acculturate the area until it took on the culture of Rome.

Unfortunately, we have relegated the meaning of *ekklesia* to merely a building, religious meeting or a social gathering of Christians. We have lost much of what the Lord wants to release through His people because we have lost the meaning of *church*, of *ekklesia*. As His ones "called out" of society, both through prayer and action, we are meant to establish the policies of God's Kingdom and declare war on injustice! "Now the manifold wisdom of God might be made known by the [*ekklesia*] to the principalities and powers in the heavenly places" (Ephesians 3:10 NKJV).

Lou Engle, speaking about the Contending House of Prayer at a conference, said it like this:

In other words, you are being called or summoned to deliberate, legislate and exert the will of God on demonic systems, injustice and false ideologies! Sunday morning dawns. You wake up. Do you think: "I'm going to church this morning" or "I'm joining the Divine Senate"? The difference could be compared to a man in Revolutionary France saying, "I'm going to my book club" or "I've just joined the Resistance!"

We are His ruling governmental body that legislates in heavenly realms through prayer. The great thing about Christ's *ekklesia* is that it takes only two or three for the meeting to be binding, not six thousand as with the ancient Romans. And whatever we bind on earth will have been bound in heaven, and whatever we loose on earth will have been loosed in heaven (see Matthew 16:19). In other words, small is the new big!

Accordingly, as God's ruling body on earth, we go into society to be countercultural change agents. We release the influence of the Kingdom of heaven, so that the principles, morals, virtues, values and ethics of that Kingdom have an impact on society. Mark 16:15 says, "And He said to them, 'Go into all the world and *preach* the gospel to all creation'" (NASB, italics added). Matthew 28:19 says, "Go therefore and make *disciples* of all the nations, baptizing them in the name of the Father and the Son and the Holy Spirit" (NASB, italics added). Matthew 25:32 says, "And all the nations will be gathered before Him; and He will separate them from one another, as the shepherd separates the sheep from the goats" (NASB). At the end of the age, every nation will be judged by the Lord as either a sheep or goat nation with regard to how they respond to the Gospel and its messengers. And to a great measure, how our nation responds will be influenced by the ekklesia's involvement in every sector of society.

We have a mandate from the Lord to preach salvation and disciple entire cities and nations. Everywhere that God's called-out ones live and work, the people around us should feel the impact of the principles, morals, values, ethics and virtues of the Kingdom. I know we often think that discipleship happens after salvation, not before. It is often easier to disciple after someone has a salvation experience, but it most certainly can happen beforehand. Let me explain.

Marketplace Discipleship

In my career in the marketplace, I had the privilege of working alongside a very talented co-worker. He was young, sharp and on the fast track within the company. As we became friends, he let me know that he did not share my faith. He stated adamantly that he did not need Christ in his life, and felt that everyone, regardless of religious beliefs, was going to heaven. Another Christian co-worker and I prayed earnestly for his salvation.

Surprisingly, though, on a weekly basis over a span of one and a half years, he asked about and engaged me in conversations about Jesus, and I explained the Gospel to him. Until this day, he still has not accepted Christ as his Lord and Savior. Within that year and a half, however, he and I began to hold each other accountable for our work ethic and for how we treated our customers. We held each other accountable particularly for the way we interacted with women who sat in private meetings with us. Customers loved us because of our customer-service approach: going above and beyond the call of duty with the utmost level of integrity. During this time, he came to embrace a pro-life stance, and he also married his girlfriend with whom he had lived for several years. The Bible also became his favorite book to read.

I believe my friend is on another fast track: the one to heaven. Although he has not yet received salvation, in the process of our time together, he (and that workplace) was discipled by the principles, morals, ethics, virtues and values of the Kingdom.

This happened because my other co-worker and I, the *ekklesia* in the workplace, observed both Mark 16:15 and Matthew 28:19 in the marketplace.

I should mention that other spiritual gatekeepers in that workplace supported New Age beliefs as well as other religions and lifestyles, but the enemy's influence did not prevail. The lives of all who worked and did business there felt the impact of the Kingdom in some way, and some even accepted Christ in their hearts.

Listen. If you are the only Christian in your workplace or company, just think: You are the highest spiritual authority for Jesus in the company! And as God's representative, you will find that co-workers will come to you. Just as non-Christian children who are raised by Christian parents can be discipled by the principles and precepts of God's Kingdom, so can unbelieving co-workers in our workplaces. This should not, of course, happen only in a place of business; it should be happening in the governments and economies of nations, as the *ekklesia* rises up to influence laws and policies by discipling the people who write, decide on and enforce them.

Subcultures and Countercultures

Ed Silvoso, in his book *Anointed for Business* (Gospel Light, 2009), points out that most of the miracles, signs and wonders Jesus performed were not in the Temple but, rather, in the marketplace, where everyone experienced life. Not only this, but when Jesus called the twelve disciples, He chose people who were not part of the religious establishment. He chose men like Matthew (a tax collector), Peter (a fisherman) and Mark (a wealthy son of inheritance). Paul, who was later added as an apostle, had his own business of building tents. None of the first twelve apostles was a religious professional; all were marketplace people. Ed writes:

> Jesus intentionally recruited marketplace people who were not members of the religious establishment because His objective was to create a new social vehicle—the Church, a movement that was meant to be the counterculture, rather than a subculture.

Every culture has a base, which is determined by the situations or circumstances of the people within it. And within that base, two subgroups of the culture usually form: These are *subcultures* and *countercultures*. As we examine these two groups we begin to see that the Church is largely missing the objective Jesus intended for us to have within society.

Webster's defines *subculture* as "an ethnic, regional, economic or social group exhibiting characteristic patterns of behavior sufficient to distinguish it from others within an embracing culture or society." Generally, subcultures (especially negative ones) are self-absorbed. They consider themselves to be outside mainstream society, and usually empower the low self-esteem of their insecure members by promoting rebellion. Their "anti the establishment" movements tear down or deconstruct the main culture. Subcultures are distinct because their members want uniqueness; their self-expression is opposite that of the main culture.

As a result, subcultures attract followers who feel rejected by society, who are searching for identity, acceptance and affirmation. Some support horrible extremes. Kids in depressing subcultures, such as emo and goth, for example, attempt to express their emotional pain by cutting themselves and having extreme piercings. This helps us understand why most negative subcultures are birthed: because of some lack or deficit in a person's life, especially a father's validation.

The definition of *counterculture* might sound at first like more of the same, but it is actually quite different. Webster defines *counterculture* as "a subgroup within culture having values and customs that are very different from and usually opposed to those accepted by most of society." Countercultures are different from subcultures in that they develop a systematic way of approaching change in the mainstream culture, and try to influence it.

In the spirit realm, subcultures and countercultures are the driving, opposing forces of influence on the earth. The spiritual subculture is the kingdom of darkness, run by its rebel leader, Satan. Because of man's fall, all the world systems lie in the power of the evil one (see 1 John 5:19), as he is the god of this age, the spirit that works in the sons of disobedience (see Ephesians 2:2). Satan, therefore, controls much of the world systems affecting politics, economies and cultures in the natural.

Satan uses subcultures in the natural realm to create intense, passionate followers. Once he identifies the best and brightest among them, he uses them to start countercultural movements that bring rapid change within nations. Most people are deceived; however, a few know exactly whom they are working for. The hippie subculture, for example, became a counterculture—the sexual revolution. One outcome of this was abortion as a law of the land in fewer than twenty years! Unbeknownst to their followers, however, many leaders of the sexual revolution, like Timothy Leary, Alfred Kinsey, Harry Hay, L. Ron Hubbard and Kenneth Anger, were followers of Aleister Crowley's occult teachings.

You see, Satan, through his one-third subgroup of unseen fallen angels or demons, seeks to hinder the Lord's plan of salvation and take humans into hell with him. He uses his human agents to tear down or deconstruct any culture in the natural that embraces the values of the Kingdom of heaven. Because man is a free-will agent, he can choose to follow Satan's agenda for death—or God's plans for life.

The good news is that in the spirit realm, the dominant culture is the Kingdom of heaven run by Jesus Christ. The Lord, through His unseen angels and visible human agents, seeks to influence laws and governments in cultures within nations. He does this to provide the opportunity for people to experience salvation, receive eternal life and further the values of His Kingdom. This invisible Kingdom is represented in the natural by the *ekklesia*, the Church. By definition, because the Church opposes the kingdoms of this world systematically and seeks to disciple nations, as heaven's representative, it is a counterculture.

It is Christ's will that none should perish, and that society should benefit from the righteous values, justice and morals of His Kingdom. Christ's followers are to proclaim the Good News of His victory on the cross, set captives free and influence society. This is our Great Commission (see Mark 16:15).

> For many years, the Church might have looked like a counterculture, but we operated like a subculture.

But this is where the problem lies: The Church has operated more as a subculture within society. We have, for instance, developed our own language, our own jargon that keeps us separate from the world. We are consumed with our own identity within the four walls of our buildings, and we are unconcerned with what is happening outside. In many regards, we foster an escapist mentality and try to avoid the people Jesus died to save! For many years, the Church might have looked like a counterculture, but we operated like a subculture. Our counterculture engagement could use a major overhaul.

James Hunter talks of three ways the Church has tried to engage the culture to effect change: "Defensive Against," "Purity From" and "Relevant To." Though he applies these terms a little differently in his book *To Change the World* (Oxford University Press, 2010), they helped me to frame, within the demographic of Church life, how most Christians approach being countercultural. You might see yourself in one of these three categories.

The first is the "Defensive Against" approach. These Christians are wearing war paint and battle armor, and slugging it out with anyone who opposes biblical principles—particularly in the courts. Though we need these warriors, some of them take a stance that makes it hard for us to reach the people they are warring against. We are called to judge certain matters, but we need to do so without being judgmental.

The next approach comes from the "Purity From" crowd. In my Christian experience, this would be the prayer movement (houses of prayer, spiritual warfare prayer groups, campus prayer groups, etc.), discernment ministry, river stream and revival folks. The main focus of this group is to stay a pure spotless Bride and pray to bring in revival. They engage the world's culture and those within it sparingly, except when God's manifest power is present. The problem here is this leads to more of a subculture mentality, if unchecked. Though it has a counterculture framework, by the time people leave their prayer closets, they are so self-absorbed within the identity of their group that they engage society with a subcultural mentality; consequently, the mainstream is turned off by their lingo, their inability to communicate and their unwillingness to relate to them. For some, the isolation has made them more religious than holy. Instead of helping people be compelled by the Church, they are making people be repelled by the Church.

The third way is the "Relevant To" approach. This would be the mega-church mentality that tries to use the greatest amount of favor to reach the broadest number of people. It usually goes to one extreme or the other. The axiom is true that the shallower your message, the larger your audience; and the deeper your message, the smaller your audience. This group is great with understanding and utilizing fads and trends in society. The leaders would make good politicians because they know how to have a broad appeal, which, by the way, is why politicians are drawn to their congregations and do well speaking to them. The problem with this approach is the tendency to become culturally relevant, instead of biblically relevant, especially in front of the major media outlets. An example of this leaning to cultural relevance is the Universalist doctrine currently embraced by some leaders, which declares that all people are going to heaven, whether or not they repent before God.

Our opinions might change, but the Word of God does not. Jack Hayford once said that when the Church tries to become contemporary, it will eventually become temporary. This is because fads and cultural trends change. Then during times of crisis, when Christians could be strategic as statesmen, we are silent because we do not want to risk losing our access within society. Martin Luther King Jr. said, "At the end of our lives, it will not be the words of our enemies that wound us most, but rather, it will be the silence of our friends." These are the ones who see church attendance as the priority, not discipleship. As a result, they sacrifice Kingdom discipleship on the altar of being "liked" on Facebook.

> When the Church tries to become contemporary, it will eventually become temporary.

That being said, all of these—"Defensive Against," "Purity From" and "Relevant To"—are like spokes within a wheel: They are necessary. But we must learn to take a stand without being judgmental, spiritually arrogant, isolationist or absorbed into culture. At the same time, we must recognize that overt as well as covert means must be employed, without finger-pointing. Is there a way to embody all of these elements to engage culture, without diluting our biblical convictions or identity?

The answer is yes.

No Longer Lepers

We can be thankful that Kingdom impact within cultures around the world is changing. The *ekklesia* is arising that Jesus Christ might receive the reward of His suffering. It is God's desire to change lives through His countercultural *ekklesia*, as believers advance the Kingdom, which makes them productive and relevant in society. We see a good example of this in Luke 5:12–15 (NKJV):

> And it happened when He was in a certain city, that behold, a man who was full of leprosy saw Jesus; and he fell on his face and implored Him, saying, "Lord, if You are willing, You can make me clean." Then He put out His hand and touched him, saying, "I am willing; be cleansed." Immediately the leprosy left him. And He charged him to tell no one, "But go and show yourself to the priest, and make an offering for your cleansing, as a testimony to them, just as Moses commanded." However, the report went around concerning Him all the more; and great multitudes came together to hear, and to be healed by Him of their infirmities.

This is an amazing story. There is more to this story than a man being healed of leprosy; rather, this is a story of a person from a subculture being healed and restored to society. In this time period, leprosy was a devastating disease. Because lepers could not feel pain, many times they were covered with wounds.

They had to watch being too close to open flames, for instance, because they could not feel fire. Everywhere they went, they had to shout, "Unclean! Unclean!" This was to warn of their presence in order to keep the disease from spreading. Anyone who came within five feet of a leper was considered unclean and had to endure a meticulous cleansing process in order to be allowed back into Temple life. When people saw lepers coming, they ran in the opposite direction.

Can you imagine how humiliating it was to shout "Unclean!" over and over again? How rejected they must have felt? At first, it concerned their medical condition, but over time *unclean* became part of their identity. As a result, lepers lived together with other lepers in colonies. For the Jews, the Temple was the center of the marketplace, social life and mainstream culture, and the leper was not part of it. The leper colony was a subculture of people who felt rejected by society.

When this leper saw Jesus, he called out, "If You are willing, I can be clean." And Jesus replied, "I am willing; be cleansed." The word *willing* in this verse really conveys God's heart toward this person who was bound to the subculture of lepers. The Lord could have used a word for *willing* that means "to make a decision based on a set of options," but the word that Jesus used means "unforced and voluntary, of one's own accord." In other words, He said, "I want to heal you; I don't have to think about it. I want to heal you now." Jesus prayed for the man, and the leprosy left! He was completely healed! Jesus did not want him just to be healed, however; he wanted him restored to the place where he could function within society. How did he accomplish this?

Jesus told the ex-leper, "Don't say anything to anybody. Go to the priest, and let him declare you healed." Why did He do this? The only way the ex-leper could be restored back into Temple life and Jewish society was by being declared clean by the priest. Because the religious hierarchy hated Jesus so much, if the leper revealed that he had been cleansed by Jesus, it is likely that the priest would not have declared him clean. Here, Jesus employs covert means as a strategy, making Himself of no reputation, so that His Father would receive glory, and a man could be restored in every way.

What do I mean? Because he followed the Lord's instructions, not only was this ex-leper delivered from leprosy, he was restored back into Temple life. Because he followed the Lord's instructions, the leper could reenter the marketplace and mainstream culture. He was now able to get a job, no longer had to beg for money and was able to function in society. His dignity was restored! Family and friends who were not allowed to touch him could embrace him for the first time, and years of rejection were broken. No longer unclean, his cleansed soul was free to worship God and tell of His marvelous works. He was set free from the subculture of a leper colony, and became an ex-leper who showed God's transforming power to the world.

God wants to do the same thing for people bound by today's "leper colony"—whether it is a music subculture or a drug subculture or a sex-trafficking, human slavery subculture. Like the leper, many are bound by hopelessness and rejection. Many are numbed by the pain of life because they have seen and experienced too much, too soon. They think they have been burned and wounded by life so much that they cannot feel anymore. Because of the way they look and dress, society calls them *thugs, gangstas, unclean.* When people see them coming, they go in the opposite direction. They are a subculture of fatherless rejects, longing for truth and a loving embrace.

To them, Jesus does not say, "Let Me think about healing you." No, He says, "I am willing. I want to heal you. I don't have to think about this; I want to heal you now." When these individuals are healed, their transformation is so powerful they do not resemble their subcultures any longer. God heals them of their wounds and makes them productive in mainstream society for the benefit of His Kingdom. Because they have been changed from the inside, the outside changes as well. Instead of curse words, they speak blessed words. And when other lepers from their former subculture see the hope in their eyes and their love for life and God, they will ask, "What must I do to get what you have?" And the ex-leper can introduce them to Jesus.

It is interesting that though this leper was told not to say a word, his story went far and wide and, according to the Bible, everyone heard about it. God wanted this man to become a sermon that everyone could see. Once you are no longer unclean, everyone will know. I believe many will soon be coming out of their subcultures and become Kingdom representatives in Christ's counterculture.

Engaging the Seven Mountains of Influence

Much has been said and written about the seven mountains of influence in society, which are family, religion, education, government, business, media, and arts and entertainment. This was first talked about when Loren Cunningham and Bill Bright met, excited to share with each other what God was saying to them about societal transformation. When they shared their notes, they were surprised that both had the same revelation regarding seven mountains or seven molders of influence in society. Biblically, mountains represent seats of authority. Since Cunningham and Bright's chance encounter in the '70s, the seven mountains idea re-emerged in Christian circles around 2001.

Today, the Seven Mountains Mandate teaching has mixed reviews. One criticism is that many who espouse the teaching are more theorists than practitioners. Others claim it is the only way to advance the Kingdom of Jesus Christ before His return.

This latter idea has led to the biggest criticism that the teaching is an exercise in dominion theology. Personally, I do not agree with a Kingdom dominion theology, with its "name it, claim it; blab it and grab it" ideals. Also, I do not adhere to some form of religious statehood, which echoes a Christianized form of sharia law. On the other hand, neither do I advocate being separatists and isolationists, who merely point fingers and curse the darkness within society, instead of being burning lamps of God's truth and love. We are called to "Go ye therefore," not "Stay ye therefore." We are called to be in the world, yet not of it (see John 17:14–17). We are called to be insulated from the world, not isolated from it. If we do not disciple our cities and nations, the enemy will.

The Jesus Movement of the late 1960s and early 1970s, for example, was one of the most sweeping movements in America. During the "hippie" years of the 1960s, God answered the cry of many mothers who were praying for the salvation of their sons and daughters. A generation that was disillusioned with societal change and war finally made the migration from the false love of the hippie movement and sexual revolution, to the true love of Jesus. Churches like Calvary Chapel in Costa Mesa, California, led by Chuck Smith, were baptizing young people in lakes and oceans by the thousands. The charismatic renewal grew during this time period, and the gifts of the Spirit began to operate more and more.

Dutch Sheets, former executive director of Christ For The Nations Institute, made a powerful observation about this in a lecture given there. He said that due to lack of fathering, the Jesus Movement fell short of going from the Mark 16:15 salvation of souls into the next level of Matthew 28:19, discipling the nation. In the meantime, a small radical fringe rose from its position as a subculture in the sexual revolution and became a counterculture, invading education, arts, media, government and other mountains of influence. Of this Dutch observed that, while the church did its version of Mark 16:15, the devil did his version of Matthew 28:19, and discipled America.

That being said, how do we engage society to make lasting change?

> "Thus says the LORD of hosts, the God of Israel, to all the exiles whom I have sent into exile from Jerusalem to Babylon, 'Build houses and live in them; and plant gardens and eat their produce. Take wives and become the fathers of sons and daughters, and take wives for your sons and give your daughters to husbands, that they may bear sons and daughters; and multiply there and do not decrease. Seek the welfare of the city where I have sent you into exile, and pray to the LORD on its behalf; for in its welfare you will have welfare.'"
>
> Jeremiah 29:4–7 NASB

When we look at Jeremiah 29, we love to skip to verse 11, which says, "'For I know the plans that I have for you,' declares the LORD, 'plans for welfare and not for calamity to give you a future and a hope.'" We forget, however, that this Scripture was spoken for people who were taken into Babylon against their will. Hananiah prophesied that they would be there for two years; Jeremiah said that they would be there for seventy years. Although God's plan was for them to return to Jerusalem, they needed a strategy for occupying their land of captivity for at least two generations. For this reason, God told them to buy houses, develop farmlands, marry and have many children. They were admonished to increase, and not to decrease, in part because the Babylonians were practicing child sacrifice—killing their offspring to appease false gods. They also needed to increase their numbers because they were the people who would repopulate Jerusalem in seventy years. In the meantime, then, how were they to engage a Babylonian culture that had destroyed their homeland and was hostile to their way of life?

In Jeremiah 29:7, the prophet presented the means for accomplishing this. God told the Israelites to pray for and actively seek the welfare of the city. The word *welfare* in this verse is the Hebrew word *shalom*, which is sometimes translated "peace." *Shalom* is an all-encompassing word that means not only "peace" but also "welfare, healing, prosperity, favor and restoration." Literally it means "nothing missing, nothing broken." Since being in Babylon for a season was part of God's plan for them, then it would do well for them to pray for its peace. For the captive Israelites, praying for the peace of the cities they were in also brought peace to them.

On this subject, James Davidson Hunter, executive director of the Institute for Advanced Studies in Culture, and author of *To Change the World: The Irony, Tragedy, and Possibility of Christianity in the Late Modern World* (Oxford University Press, 2010), writes,

> Clearly it would have been justifiable for the Jews to be hostile to their captors. It also would have been natural enough for them to withdraw from engaging the world around them. By the same token, it would have been easy for them to simply assimilate with the culture that surrounded them. Any of these three options made sense in human terms. But God was calling them to something different—not to be defensive against, isolated from, or absorbed into the dominant culture, but to be faithfully present within it. On the face of it, this was not a posture of radical and prophetic challenge to the powers that be, but neither was it a passive acceptance of the established order. The people of Israel were being called to enter the culture in which they were placed as God's people—reflecting in their daily practices their distinct identity as those chosen by God. He was calling them to maintain their distinctiveness as a community but in ways that served the common good.

What a powerful observation! Israel was called to be a holy nation within a vile culture, to live differently while meeting the needs of those around them. Faithfulness for them was seeking to be a blessing, even as exiles in a hostile environment.

Taking Responsibility

In the New Testament, we are called to live out this Old Testament reality. Today, God is at work in our "exile," and our peace is tied to the peace we release to the cities we live in. First Peter 3:17 encourages us that "it is better . . . to suffer for doing good than for doing evil." We are also admonished to "look out for the interest of others, and not your own." Paul also says in 1 Corinthians 12:7, "Now to each one the manifestation of the Spirit is given for the common good." Whether our presence is treated with disdain, hostility or ingratitude, God's mandate to us is to be committed to the shalom of our cities. In Jeremiah's day, Israel's hope was their return to the city of Jerusalem. In like manner, this place is not our home; a New Jerusalem, coming down from heaven, will be our new home (see Revelation 21:10). We need to populate that city with new family members in Christ. We are to increase, not decrease. Unto that end, we share the Gospel and disciple nations, "for He knows the plans He has for us."

Work, worship and culture are intertwined in our lives. I find it fascinating that *work* and *worship* are both derived from the same Hebrew word *avodah*. Worship was never meant to be an event, but a lifestyle. Of this, Os Hillman writes in *Change Agent: Engaging Your Passion to Be the One Who Makes a Difference* (Charisma, 2011): "We are to view our work as worship to God. All of life should be conducted as a form of worship. When the Olympic runner Eric Liddell described his gift of running to his sister in the classic film *Chariots of Fire*, he said,

'When I run, I feel His pleasure.' We too should feel His pleasure when we work unto Him."

We see this with Cain and Abel. They did not offer musical gestures before God in a temple; rather, they offered their work as worship to God. Abel offered up his best work, while his brother offered up, well, his "not so best" work. Cain's jealousy of Abel drove him to murder. Ever wonder why people get a little jealous of you at work? It is because wholehearted work is worship, and when it is offered up to God, it is powerful.

When we work, we are participating in the act of cultivating. In Genesis 2:15 we read that God gave Adam the charge to cultivate the earth. The word *culture*, remember, comes from the word *cultivate*. As we work, we are tilling the soil of society, cultivating culture with the artifacts, knowledge and other resources provided us by God. As a matter of fact, culture is the ultimate expression of who or what society worships. Culture comes from the Latin word *cultus*, which, you guessed it, means "adoration or worship." Creating and cultivating are part of our divine mandates from God as we co-labor or work with Him in shaping culture. This frames the world in which we live as a lifestyle of worship.

Unto that end, we pray for the cities in which we live, because within them are the people who have latent redeemed potential to offer up praise to God. They also are bestowed with common grace, and God uses their skills and abilities to better society and further His plans, even in their unredeemed state. We see this when God used Cyrus, who was not a follower of Jehovah, to usher Israel back to Jerusalem when the seventy years had ended (see Isaiah 44:28). As believers, we contribute our labor within our cities to make society better, so that others are benefactors of the precepts and principles of the Kingdom of heaven. Is God concerned about where we live? Our culture? Do our prayers have any effect on the outcome of the commerce of cities?

On March 28, 2000, the city of Fort Worth, Texas, was hit with an F-3 category tornado, killing three people as it went through the heart of the city. One of the buildings damaged was the downtown Bank One Tower building. Though this is not a city known for its skyscrapers, this building was a familiar cultural landmark on Fort Worth's skyline. Downtown Fort Worth was in the middle of being revitalized, and, suddenly, one of its most important cultural artifacts was threatened. Just when many residents thought someone would buy the building and renovate it, Bank One decided not to recommit to being the lead tenant in the building and abandoned downtown.

During a time of prayer and fasting after the tornado, God broke my heart for the city of my birth. I felt impressed by the Lord to consider this building as the heart of the city of Fort Worth. I sensed the Lord saying, "Let's consider the soul of the city, and seek its welfare." I prayed Jeremiah 29:7 and during the next 21 days, I walked around the abandoned, boarded-up high-rise, praying for God to restore it as a sign of heart restoration and salvation for people within the city of Fort Worth. I informed other intercessors and they prayed with me, and I am sure that others were praying for our city as well.

> We pray for the cities in which we live, because within them are the people who have latent redeemed potential to offer up praise to God.

Shortly after the fast, as a confirmation, the local newspaper released an article saying exactly what we were hearing in prayer. They ran a picture of the dilapidated building, with a caption underneath that read: "Let's Consider the Soul of the City." In the article, both the mayor and the president of the convention bureau at that time spoke about the negative impact of an unoccupied, 35-story building downtown. On top of the one thousand jobs already lost in Fort Worth, another company was relocating in Houston, taking eight hundred more jobs. This dormant high-rise would prove to be either Fort Worth's demise or her redemption.

Months went by, and it seemed all hope was lost. Then a purchaser came forward with a plan to renovate it! The city council and structural engineers approved the plan, and the bank building was transformed into high-rise apartments. Today, it is fully occupied and teeming with life! Downtown Fort Worth has become the rival of cities nationally. Clean, safe and family-friendly, downtown Fort Worth's nightlife and economic life were restored.

Though some could argue that our prayers for the cultural life of a city were of no concern to God, the truth is that we will live eternally in a new Jerusalem, a city coming down from heaven. It will be teeming with cultural life for the redeemed living in its dwelling places. Remember, the one Jesus said He was going away to prepare for us? Revelation 21:9–11 (KJV) says,

> And there came unto me one of the seven angels which had the seven vials full of the seven last plagues, and talked with me, saying, Come hither, I will shew thee the bride, the Lamb's wife. And he carried me away in the spirit to a great and high mountain, and shewed me that great city, the holy Jerusalem, descending out of heaven from God, having the glory of God: and her light was like unto a stone most precious, even like a jasper stone, clear as crystal.

In *Culture Making: Recovering Our Creative Calling* (Inter-Varsity, 2013), Andy Crouch writes,

> But the end of humanity as depicted in Revelation is more than a temple— an everlasting worship service. In fact, as we've seen, a temple is the one notable thing the new Jerusalem does not have (Rev 21:22). The new Jerusalem needs no temple because every

aspect of life in that city is permeated with the light and love of God. In that sense worship as we know it . . . will be obsolete. What will take its place? The most plausible answer, it seems to me, is that our eternal life in God's recreated world will be the fulfillment of what God originally asked us to do: cultivating and creating in full and lasting relationship with our Creator. This time, of course, we will not just be tending a garden; we will be sustaining the life of a city, a harmonious human society that has developed all the potentialities hidden in the original creation to their fullest. Culture—redeemed, transformed and permeated by the presence of God—will be the activity of eternity.

Unto that end, we pray, cultivate and create within our communities, sharing the Gospel and living it out in our daily lives, actively engaged in the problems in our cities, redeeming hearts and artifacts at the same time, in preparation for inhabiting the holy city that will come down from heaven.

The Critical Place of Intercession

For centuries Jews and Christians have obeyed the biblical injunction to pray for the peace of Jerusalem. Our responsibility, however, does not end there. During her exile, God called Israel to get involved in the life of Babylon, actively to seek the shalom of the city until nothing was missing and nothing was broken. In this way, they were not just a voting block, but also problem solvers for society. We, too, must take responsibility for developing and implementing solutions to the issues within our societies. Influence follows those who take responsibility, and it usually starts with prayer to hear God's heart on the matter.

Being an intercessor is critical for being effective in the marketplace if we hope to reclaim the seven mountains. Intercession is focused prayer and involvement that takes responsibility by standing in the gap or exposed places until heaven's resources reach the earth (see Ezekiel 22:30). We allow God to break our hearts over things that break His heart, showing us what needs to be addressed in culture, what areas He is placing His finger on. In this way, we carry God's heart while carrying out our marketplace endeavors.

For a good example, look at this passage that talks about God's heart for justice, for making things right. Isaiah 59:15–16 (NASB) says,

> Yes, truth is lacking; and he who turns aside from evil makes himself a prey. Now the LORD saw, and it was displeasing in His sight that there was no justice. And He saw that there was no man, and was astonished that there was no one to intercede; then His own arm brought salvation to Him.

Take note of two very important words in these verses: *displeasing* and *astonished*. In Hebrew, these words reveal God's heart over injustice. *Displeasing* is the word *raa*, which means "to spoil something by breaking it into pieces." The Hebrew word for *astonished* is *shamem*, which means "to devastate, to amaze, to stun or to grow numb." Think of it: When the Creator of the universe sees injustice, His heart is broken. He then seeks someone on earth to share this burden with Him in intercession and bring relief to His heart. When He cannot find anyone who is concerned about injustice, He is astonished, stunned and devastated!

> We allow God to break our hearts over things that break His heart, showing us what needs to be addressed in culture, what areas He is placing His finger on.

The word *justice* in this verse is *mishpat*, which means "a verdict announced judicially," especially a sentence or formal decree. Whether the lack of justice is legalized racist decrees, such as the Dred Scott decision during the years of slavery in America, along with the Jim Crow segregation laws, or legalized death decrees, such as abortion and euthanasia, it is God's desire to have intercessors be moved by His heart and, through prayer and action, release His Kingdom justice on earth.

On the cross, Jesus brought about eternal justice for the Father regarding our sin, granting eternal life for those who receive the gift of salvation. God is now looking for us to get involved in the exposed, vulnerable places within society, and stand in the gap for Him. Ezekiel 22:30 (NASB) says, "I searched for a man among them who would build up the wall and stand in the gap before Me for the land, so that I would not destroy it; but I found no one."

God is still looking for intercessors to comfort His heart. How shattered His heart must be, not only over injustice, but over human trafficking, slavery, poverty, fatherlessness—the list goes on! It is interesting: We are astonished at the lack of power in the Church, yet God is astonished that there is no intercessor. No intercession, no power. God is looking for intercessors whose hearts are shattered to pieces in deep travail over the needs of their day.

I want to share with you three examples of individuals who heard God's heart for brokenness in the marketplace and stood in the gap. These entrepreneurs were used by God to meet the needs of society, and by doing so funded the advancement of His Kingdom.

Kingdom Entrepreneurs

God is raising up Kingdom entrepreneurs. *Entrepreneur* describes a person involved in starting new business venture, to meet the needs of society. We might not think, however, of entrepreneurs and new business enterprises as tools used by God to fund the advancement of His Kingdom.

The word *entrepreneur* is made of two root words. *Entre* means "to go between," as to be involved in a business undertaking. One meaning of *prendre* is "to undertake." As you can see from these two roots, an entrepreneur is a person who gets involved in a business undertaking, who goes between a problem and a solution in terms of goods or services. This sounds a lot like the definition of an intercessor!

So, what does it look like when intercessors become entrepreneurs and their businesses stand in the gap? Let's take a look at three stories that answer that question.

An Intercessor's Dream

Madame C. J. Walker was born just after slavery in America ended, but she lived a very hard life. She grew up illiterate and worked as a washerwoman well into her thirties. Despite being born free, her early life was not easy. Her parents both died before she was eight, and she was forced to work in the cotton fields to survive. At the age of fourteen, she moved to Vicksburg, Louisiana, and married Moses McWilliams, who died in 1887 just two years after the birth of their daughter Lelia. She worked as a cook and laundress before marrying John Davis in 1894, who abused her. The couple separated in 1903, and she and her daughter moved to St. Louis, Missouri.

While in St. Louis, Madame C. J. Walker suffered from a scalp infection that caused most of her hair to fall out. Other African American women she worked with had the same thing happen to them. As a result, she began experimenting with various medicines and hair products, but nothing seemed to work.

As she prayed and interceded for an answer to their need, God gave her a dream. She described it this way:

God answered my prayer, for one night I had a dream, and in that dream a big, black man appeared to me and told me what to mix up in my hair. Some of the remedy was grown in Africa, but I sent for it, mixed it, put it on my scalp, and in a few weeks my hair was coming in faster than it had ever fallen out. I tried it on my friends; it helped them. I made up my mind to begin to sell it.

Walker did indeed begin selling the product. Much has been written about how, defying all odds, she learned to read and write, mastered marketing concepts, and built a booming cosmetics empire that provided lucrative work for thousands of black women and allowed her to engage in philanthropy and civil rights activism until her death in a Westchester mansion in 1919.

Walker made millions on her "Wonderful Hair Grower." She is cited by Guinness World Records as being not only the first black woman millionaire, but also the first American female self-made millionaire. She began a hair care business that made her fortune, a feat unheard of for any woman at that time, let alone a woman of color.

Madame C. J. Walker was an awesome Christian woman who funded the spread of the Gospel in Africa, planted churches and orphanages, gave toward education for African Americans, and helped fund the American civil rights movement in its inception.

As you can see, this intercessor was given a dream in answer to her prayer, then God used her to answer His dream of justice for the poor and marginalized. Her business "went between" social problems and answers, releasing the justice of the Kingdom. This intercessor became an entrepreneur who stood in the gap with her business. (See more of Madam C. J. Walker's story at http://inventors.about.com/od/wstartinventors/a/MadameWalker_2.htm, last accessed December 9, 2013; and http://www.madamewalker.net/History/tabid/537/Default.aspx, last accessed December 9, 2013.)

Giving Poverty the Boot

I heard Sam Bistrian speak not long ago at Christ For The Nations Institute. Sam told how he was raised in Transylvania. His fondest memory of growing up was receiving a pair of rain boots when he was six years old. Sam was one of twelve brothers and sisters, and the pair of hand-me-down boots meant the world to him. People in his village suffered from frostbite, and many lost toes because their feet were not protected in the cold rainy weather. Other times of year, the lack of shoes meant the rapid spread of malaria and other diseases among young and old. Not having proper footwear compounded health problems in his community, and such, he explained, is the case globally, for people who live in wetland areas.

Over time, the Gospel came to Sam's family and his parents became Christians. This was around the time that Communism fell. When Sam's father died, the family left for the United States and started life over in Chicago. Before long, Sam and a few other siblings decided to go to Christ For The Nations Institute Bible school. Sam focused on a missions major and held a job with a large airliner.

His next job was at a high-end clothing store in Dallas, Texas, within the shoe department. Because of his work ethic, Sam soon became manager of the shoe department. In the meantime, he was able to pursue certain missionary work in various countries because part of his severance package with his earlier job at the airline included flight benefits.

One day, Sam met the founder of a shoe company that had a policy of giving shoes to the poor. Sam mentioned to this man the problem poor people face in the wetlands around the world and suggested he offer rain boots through his company. The man looked at Sam and said, "Why don't you do it?" That question lit a spark within Sam. From his knowledge in the fashion industry, he eventually designed a stylish rain boot for women and purposed to donate one pair to the poor for every pair sold.

He went to banks with his idea, but none would lend him the money. He then sold his car and other items and borrowed money from friends and family. He used his flight benefits to meet with manufacturers, and eventually cut the right deal to manufacture ten thousand pairs of boots: five thousand to sell, and another five thousand to give away.

The company, Roma Boots, took off. Sam was able to give away thousands of rain boots in the Transylvanian village where he grew up. He is also working with his sister who runs an orphanage there. They are spreading the love of Jesus and, as their slogan says, "Giving poverty the boot" every time they sell a pair of shoes. Roma has been featured nationally, and Sam has been a guest speaker at various schools talking about social entrepreneurship. (See more at www.romaboots.com.)

Hairdressers in the Marketplace

Hairstylist Teresa Russo-Cox founded Hairdressers in the Marketplace (HIM) in 1998 after unsuccessfully trying numerous volunteer positions at her large church. Nothing seemed to fit until God gave her a vision for a ministry that reaches out to women in need. Now, one day a month, a group of professionals armed with blow dryers, scissors and nail polish venture forth to help those less fortunate.

These "Day of Beauty" sessions offer free haircuts and manicures to women in need. HIM volunteers also go to nursing homes, homeless shelters and facilities for the mentally disabled to provide free services. While sharing God's love with those who might not have an opportunity to receive this special attention, HIM also communicates God's care to those working in the beauty industry itself.

Teresa and her volunteers are bringing the light of God's Word into the marketplace, and showing His love to those who long to feel special, inside and out. (Read her story at www .todayschristianwoman.com.)

True Christianity

Various writings from the second and third centuries reveal what Christian life was like within the world and how Christians aspired to live. The following is a passage from an unknown disciple of the apostles, writing a defense, or description, of Christianity to Diognetus. (See http://www.earlychristian writings.com/text/diognetus-roberts.html.)

> For the Christians are distinguished from other men neither by country, nor language, nor the customs which they observe. For they neither inhabit cities of their own, nor employ a peculiar form of speech, nor lead a life which is marked out by any singularity. . . . But, inhabiting Greek as well as barbarian cities, according as the lot of each of them has determined, and following the customs of the natives in respect to clothing, food, and the rest of their ordinary conduct, they display to us their wonderful and confessedly striking method of life. They dwell in their own countries, but simply as sojourners. . . . They marry, as do all [others]; they beget children; but they do not destroy their offspring. . . . They obey the prescribed laws, and at the same time surpass the laws by their lives. They love all men, and are persecuted by all. They are unknown and condemned; they are put to death, and restored to life. They are poor, yet make many rich; they are in lack of all things, and yet abound in all. . . . They are evil spoken of, and yet are justified; they are reviled, and bless; they are insulted, and repay the insult with honour; they do good, yet are punished as evil-doers. When punished, they rejoice as if quickened into life; they are assailed by the Jews as foreigners, and are persecuted by the Greeks;

yet those who hate them are unable to assign any reason for their hatred.

From this powerful ancient letter, we see the words attributed to St. Francis of Assisi, "Preach the gospel everywhere, and, if necessary, use words." Up to now, the Church has focused primarily on engaging culture through changing laws without addressing other aspects of society. The result is that the nation sees us more as a voting block than loving people who lay down their lives for Christ in their communities. A political focus leaves us biting our nails with every approaching election and wringing our hands until the next one. I am not advocating disengaging from politics; rather, I am stressing our need to reengage culture in different ways. The salvation of souls must become equally important as discipling our families, workplaces and communities in the ways of the Kingdom of heaven, by becoming sermons people see.

> The salvation of souls must become equally important as discipling our families, workplaces and communities in the ways of the Kingdom of heaven, by becoming sermons people see.

In an article entitled "Is the Religious Right Finished?" in *Christianity Today* (this was in September 1999—the same year as the study of the city of Dallas), Don Eberly commented:

Christians are understandably dismayed that the culture has become unhitched from its Judeo-Christian roots. What many refuse to acknowledge is that, in a thousand ways, this unhitching was produced by a massive retreat by Christians from the intellectual, cultural, and philanthropic life of the nation. While evangelicals count millions of members among their grassroots political groups and are now, if anything, overrepresented in the legislative arena, the number of evangelicals at the top of America's powerful culture-shaping institutions could be seated in a single school bus! The watching world is understandably chagrined by the interest evangelicals have shown in power while simultaneously showing so little interest in the noncoercive arenas of society where one's only weapon is persuasion.

As you can see, discipling the marketplace is key, for without it we will not have sustainability when we experience spiritual awakenings. Lance Wallnau points out that if we are to have a third Great Awakening, it must envelop the cultural gatekeepers of our day; otherwise, we will not get the lasting effects and tangible results seen with previous awakenings.

Wallnau said this while speaking about the Welsh Revival. He explained that although 100,000 were swept into salvation within three months, and a powerful revival spread and lasted for many years, today, 100 years later, fewer than 2 percent of people in Wales are Christians.

This happened because the cultural gatekeepers were not swept into that spiritual awakening, and, as a result, there has been no lasting fruit. This is why I believe God is sending His people into the marketplace, and some will be promoted by God to have significant impact on the mountains of influence. In doing so, we must become open to God's process for becoming a change agent. Mountains are reclaimed when we allow God to reclaim the hearts of people in leadership. We will explore this more in the next chapter.

EXERCISING INFLUENCE *through Prayer*

Father, we come before You as Your ruling governmental body, asking for Your forgiveness for how we have abdicated our responsibility to be salt and light within society. We are known more for what we are against than what You are for. Many of us are more isolated from the world than ever, instead of insulated with Your tender mercy. And some of us, in our attempts to be relevant to the world, have become absorbed within it, and no longer resemble the spotless Bride You are coming back for. For the sake of Jesus' name, and those He died to save, set us free from our self-righteous subculture mentality. We sit in astonishment, staring at the condition of our cities, yet all the while, You sit, astonished, that there are no intercessors. Father, break our hearts over the condition of our communities and restore and raise up Your ekklesia! Oh, God, we ask for divine strategies in this hour for the neighborhoods, communities and cities in which we live. Make us problem solvers to society again, a faithful presence within the world. Help us to counter the culture with Your loving embrace, to populate the New Jerusalem coming down from heaven. Thank You for the good plans You have for us to give us a future, a hope and an expected end. In Jesus' name, Amen.

11

Reclaiming the Seven Mountains and the Threshing Floor

MOUNTAINTOP LEADERS OCCUPY SEATS of authority effectively *only* when we willingly participate in the transformational process God has designed for our success. With the ascent of the "seven mountain" teaching, however, while there have been some successes, there have also been glaring misrepresentations within the various spheres of influence, which have affected the credibility of Christians as effective societal change agents.

- A son of one of the most influential gospel families in America was found guilty of racketeering—running a Ponzi scheme within the church. Many lost millions in retirement money. Three other major Ponzi schemes took place during this same time period, shaking many megachurches throughout the United States.

- A female worship pastor in a Singapore mega-church launched a secular music venture, producing a video that was as raunchy as any produced by the most licentious secular artists. Along the way, her husband was accused of embezzling more than $40 million from their church in order to fund her secular music quest in America.
- The influential National Association of Evangelicals (NAE) was rocked when its leader was exposed in a major sex and drug scandal. This not only resulted in his resignation, and being ousted from the church he founded, but opened Christians to mockery in the secular world.

Sadly, these are just a few examples, among many, of Christians called to take up seats of authority within one of the seven mountains of influence, who ended up being transformed by the world systems they initially sought to transform. While I am a proponent of some of the seven mountains teaching, I feel that in order to implement a sustainable model for achieving societal transformation, we must emphasize the process for becoming a person used by God to influence those mountains, or seats of authority, in society.

Bottom line: As a believer, if you do not allow God to sift your heart, you will become, at best, a compromising Christian with no influence on the mountain or, at worst, just like the world. We are called to be on the mountain, but not of it. The old adage is true: "Power corrupts, and absolute power, corrupts absolutely." Otherwise, we will be led astray by the spirit of harlotry on top of the seven mountains described in Revelation 17:9 (NASB): "Here is the mind which has wisdom. The seven heads are seven mountains on which the woman sits."

When Satan sees Christians who are a threat to his world system, one of the ways he attacks them is through temptation. The same tempting offer that was made to our Lord will, at some point, be made to us. Where did Satan offer to Jesus all the kingdoms of this world? On top of a mountain!

> Again, the devil took Him to a very high mountain and showed Him all the kingdoms of the world and their glory; and he said to Him, "All these things I will give You, if You fall down and worship me." Then Jesus said to him, "Go, Satan! For it is written, 'YOU SHALL WORSHIP THE LORD YOUR GOD, AND SERVE HIM ONLY.'"
>
> Matthew 4:8–10 NASB

Again, before Jesus left for Calvary, He knew that the enemy was coming to tempt Him again. He told His disciples, "I will not speak much more with you, for the ruler of the world is coming, and he has nothing in Me" (John 14:30 NASB).

Remember, the Hebrew word for "influence" is *yad*, which means "hand," and by Satan's "hand," the Lord knew Satan was coming to tempt Him, and try to transform Him before He transformed the world. Jesus' words *nothing in Me* were a reference to a handle that the enemy could grab hold of, such as sin, pride or faulty heart motives, through which the enemy could sway or influence Him. The same goes for you and me. Before we take our seats of authority regarding any of the mind molders within culture, we need to make sure the enemy has nothing in us. This is why we first must be transformed by the other precious place upon hilltops and mountains: the threshing floor.

> Before we take our seats of authority regarding any of the mind molders within culture, we need to make sure the enemy has nothing in us.

In this chapter, we will learn about how God prepares us to become the change agents He has called us to be in society. Together, we will look at biblical examples of some who went through the process and became shining examples within their spheres of influence. Let's start by understanding what a threshing floor is.

The Place Where Influence Is Processed

The threshing floor was a large flat rock on which farmers could process their wheat. These slabs, which measured up to forty feet in diameter, were generally located up in the mountaintops, and were very valuable commodities; they were even warred over by kings.

Farmers spread their wheat on the slab and ran a threshing sledge over it to separate the grain from the stalk. One variation of the threshing sledge was a long plank with handles on both sides. It had spiked wheels, broken pottery and rocks underneath, all of which helped separate the wheat kernels. The workers would push and pull the threshing sledge back and forth over and over again, creating a *shwook, shwook, shwook* sound. Another type of threshing sledge was pulled by an ox. This one was a plank with spiked wheels. The farmer and his family would stand on the plank to give it added weight.

When the grinding was finished, the farmer used a winnowing fork to throw the threshed mixture into the air. The strong mountaintop winds would carry away the chaff, while the weightier kernels of wheat would fall straight back to the ground. This is why threshing floors were built in open spaces on top of hills and mountains—so the winds could blow away the chaff. Interestingly, a kernel of wheat is shaped aerodynamically to cut through wind and go straight up and down. Since rocks also can get caught up in the mixture, the farmer eventually has to sift through the mixture to further shake and separate any stones from the wheat kernels.

The symbolism of a threshing floor is a way to understand God's dealings with His people. The threshing floor and threshing in the Bible represent God's mountaintop experience of shaking, as well as miraculous transformation in our lives, by which we are made into the image and likeness of Christ to become people of influence. The threshing floor is the place where:

- Joseph worshiped and mourned the loss of his father Jacob (see Genesis 50:10)
- Gideon encountered and tested God (see Judges 6:37)
- Ruth met Boaz, her husband-redeemer (see Ruth 3:3)
- David built an altar and God stayed His hand of judgment (see 1 Chronicles 21:15)

I find it interesting that the first time the threshing floor is talked about in the Bible, in the story of Joseph, it is not in regard to farming; rather, it is a place for mourning, brokenness and worship.

I often wondered why Joseph mourned and worshiped at the threshing floor. Then one day, it hit me: What were Joseph's dreams about? Joseph dreamed that the sun, the moon and eleven stars were bowing down to him (see Genesis 37:9). According to his father's interpretation, the sun represented his father, the moon represented his mother, and the eleven stars represented his brothers, and all were bowing down to Joseph, representing his authority over them (see Genesis 37:10). Joseph's great-grandfather Abraham was promised a people as numerous as the stars (see Genesis 15:5), and the eleven stars along with Joseph were the twelve sons of promise who became tribes that made up the nation of Israel. As you can see, this dream represented the authority Joseph would exercise over his family and the entire nation of Israel.

The sun, moon and stars also illustrate another spiritual truth about Joseph and God's plan for him. Joseph eventually became a ruler in Egypt, a "father to Pharaoh" (Genesis 45:8)—in other words, Pharaoh's most trusted advisor. Remember also, that in chapters 1 and 2 we learned that stars biblically represent the influence of God's people (see Daniel 12:3; Philippians 2:15), as well as angels (see Judges 5:20; Revelation 12:4), which many scholars believe are principalities and powers (see Ephesians 6:12). Egypt, where God was sending Joseph, worshiped the sun god, Ra, the moon goddess, Isis, and the stars and constellations that made up Orion, connected to their worship of Osiris (see Job 38:31).

In other words, this dream represented not only the authority Joseph eventually exercised over Israel, but also the authority and influence he would exercise in the heavenly realms over the angelic stars (principalities and powers) that controlled Egypt. To achieve that level of authority and influence, however, he had to go through God's process, represented by his first dream. In that night vision, Joseph dreamt that he was wheat, and that his brothers were wheat bowing down to him (see Genesis 37:7). You see, Joseph not only received a dream about being wheat, but like wheat, he had to go through a process of transformation in order to be used. So do you and I. Otherwise, instead of discipling the nations, the nations will disciple us.

Joseph: No Handle for the Enemy

Potiphar's wife was attracted to Joseph, not only for his looks. Political alliances were made back then through secret liaisons. She was not pursuing a good-looking slave, but a rising star "on the fast track." Satan knew Joseph was a threat, and undoubtedly was behind her attempt to seduce Joseph. When the spiritual powers sent Potiphar's wife to Joseph to commit adultery, he resisted, because his allegiance was to the Lord, and not the world system. The enemy came to him, but had nothing in Joseph, because he was in the world, but not of it. This brings us to one of the reasons Joseph is worshiping and mourning at a threshing floor.

More than likely, Joseph looked at the process he went through in his life: being sold into slavery by his brothers, thrown into jail, and finally reaching his destiny as the person at the right hand to the ruler of one of the most powerful kingdoms dominating the world at that time. Joseph realized that he was the wheat he saw in his dream, and like wheat, he had to go through God's threshing floor process. He was threshed through slavery, threshed by being in prison, and in the process, transformed to become a ruler in Egypt. Had the winds of adversity not had their perfect work in his life, Joseph would have never become a strong leader. Even naturally, wind is necessary for strength and growth in plants and trees. The following story from *1001 Illustrations That Connect* (Zondervan, 2009) helps to illustrate the point:

> For two years, scientists sequestered themselves in an artificial environment called Biosphere 2. Inside their self-sustaining community, the Biospherians created a number of mini-environments, including a desert, rain forest, and ocean. Nearly every weather condition could be simulated except one: wind. Over time, the effects of their windless environment became apparent. A number of acacia trees bent over and snapped. Without the stress of wind to strengthen the wood, the trunks grew weak and could not hold up their own weight. Though our culture shuns hardship, we would do well to remember that God uses hardship "for our good, that we may share in his holiness" (Hebrews 12:10).

Spiritually, winds of change come into our lives and strengthen us first through separation. God does this to pull us away from sin, so that we can pursue Him, unhindered. When people first "get saved," they are often told that their best life is now, and times will only get better. Truthfully, for most Christians, soon after the salvation experience, we experience God's purification process. We often quote the words of John the Baptist in Matthew 3:11, which says, "I baptize you with water for repentance, but He who is coming after me . . . will baptize you with the Holy Spirit and fire" (NASB). Usually, we hear that verse and say, "Yay, thank God for the Holy Ghost!" The next verse, however, says, "His winnowing fork is in His hand, and He will thoroughly clear His threshing floor." He will not stop until it is clean. In other words, after salvation comes the purification process, where the fiery trials of life are used to bring about righteousness in us. There can be no promotion or elevation, without separation. This separation process through fiery trials is necessary to help develop discipline and character in your life.

First Peter 1:6–7 says,

> In this you greatly rejoice, though now for a little while you may have had to suffer grief in all kinds of trials. These have come so that your faith—of greater worth than gold, which perishes even though refined by fire—may be proved genuine and may result in praise, glory and honor when Jesus Christ is revealed.

The Mystery of Becoming Who You Are

May I tell you a couple of secrets? Brace yourself for the first one. Ready? Here it is: There will be several times throughout your Christian life that you will encounter the threshing floor. Sometimes it will be for personal sin issues, of course, but many times that is not the case. If you let God use these hard times, and you persevere, God will take you to a greater place of intimacy and influence with Him.

The other secret is an observation I have made over many years in the marketplace. Whether they are called to the business, government or art and entertainment mountains, the Christians whom God is using effectively in these spheres have gone through a process; their reliance is not upon a person, a career status or even their positions on their mountains. As a matter of fact, many of them, though they enjoy their jobs, will tell you they do not need their jobs; they need God. For them, this is not mere rhetoric. They may possess money, fame or success, but it does not possess them. They hold money, power and fame with open palms, not clinched fists. As a result, God trusts them with affluence and influence to affect the lives of many. If you yield to a lifestyle of worship through your threshing floor process, God will use you as well beyond anything you can imagine (see Ephesians 3:20).

Remember, the threshing floor is the place where the yield is produced. You have probably heard the stock market term of a *yield* coming from a particular stock. *Yield* is actually a farming term, as with much of the language from the stock exchange. My point is this: God has an investment in you. God does not thresh weeds; He threshes wheat. You do

> God has an investment in you.

not go through this process unless you are precious to Him. So precious that He loves you too much to leave you where you are, and the way you are. The threshing floor is the place where you learn the truth about who you really are, and who you can become in Christ.

Jesus said to Simon Peter, "On this rock I will build My church, and the gates of Hades shall not prevail against it" (Matthew 16:18 NKJV). Jesus said this after asking the question, "Who do you say that I am?" Simon correctly answered, "You are the Christ, the Son of the living God." Our Savior responded by changing Simon's name to Peter, which means "little rock." And then He said, "On this rock I will build My Church" (verses 15–19). The rock was not Peter, however. The Rock is Christ, the Son of the Living God. He is the Rock of offense and stone of stumbling—like a threshing floor (see Isaiah 8:14). The Lord is our threshing floor and those who fall on the Rock shall be broken, and those whom the Rock falls on will be crushed to powder (Matthew 21:44). I would much rather be broken now than crushed later.

One day, all the nations will have to face the truth of who He is, and will bow out of adoration or humiliation. Before that great day comes, however, the Lord reveals who He really is, and who we really are, at the threshing floor. He reveals our weakness so that we may boast in His love, grace, strength and power. This is what happened with Peter.

Peter's Sifting: From Love to Greater Love

Peter said to the Lord, "I'll never deny you, and as a matter of fact, I'll die for you." The Lord responded, "Before the cock crows, you will have denied Me" (see Matthew 26:33–34). Peter was about to go to the threshing floor. Why do I say that? Jesus says in another account of this incident, "Peter, Satan has desired to sift you like wheat, but I have prayed for you" (see Luke 22:31–32). Peter had to have the remaining "Simon" (*Simon* means "shifty") threshed out of his life. Peter trusted his own ability to serve God more than God's commitment to love him even through his failures. The Lord knew what was going to happen to Peter, and He did not prevent it. Just as with Joseph, God watched over this process and used it for His glory. Peter was broken from trusting in his own strength and began trusting in God alone, trusting the God of the second chance.

Peter denied the Lord three times, and the last time, he heard the cock crow. Then the Lord turned and looked at him as if to say, "I know what is in your heart. As painful as it is to you, there is part of your heart that you cannot deny; nor can you cut it away. I must circumcise 'Simon' out of your life at the threshing floor" (see Luke 22:61). Peter ran away and wept bitterly.

(In addition to the cock crowing, he must have heard *shwook, shwook, shwook* in the background.)

Sometimes, our English language conceals the subtle nuances that are powerful expressions in the original biblical languages. You see this in Jesus and Peter's discourse in John 21:15–17. Later, when Peter encountered the risen Lord, Jesus spoke to him and said, "Simon, son of Jonah, do you love Me more than these?" (NKJV). The word the Lord used for *love* was the Greek word *agape*, which means "covenantal, unconditional love." Peter responded by saying, "Lord, You know I love You." Peter did not say *agape*, however. Peter said *phileo*, which means "brotherly love," a weaker version of love than *agape*. In other words, Peter was acknowledging his weakness before God, and his inability to love and serve Him in his own strength.

Again, the Lord asked Peter, "Do you *agape* Me?" and Peter responded, "No, I *phileo* You." The last time, the Lord said, "Peter, do you *phileo* Me?" In essence, Jesus was saying, "I'll meet you at your level, and My love for you is so strong, it will draw you into covenantal love." Peter responded, "Lord, you know all things, you know I *phileo* You."

An interesting thing happened, however. Every time Peter responded with honesty, the Lord not only called him back to ministry, but also gave him a promotion—from feeding and tending lambs to mature sheep. God promotes honest, broken people whose only hope is God's grace in their lives. Jesus was showing Peter, "It isn't the strength of your fleshly commitment that is sustaining our relationship, but the strength of My love and commitment to you. And when you bask in My overwhelming love, knowing that I see your weakness, you will serve Me with a commitment and desire beyond your wildest dreams."

From that point on, Peter was changed by the grace and love of God. He later preached the first sermon at Pentecost, at the start of the Church. And when he was killed, he asked them to crucify him upside down, saying that he was not worthy to die the same way the Lord did. "Greater love has no one than this, that he lay down his life for his friends" (John 15:13). Peter went from friendship love to covenant love, and laid down his life for his friend and Lord. The Lord knew there was a yield in Peter's life that was yet to come. Peter proved to be worth the investment, and so are you. Let this story of a pastor's threshing floor encounter encourage you.

Extracting the Precious from the Worthless

During the mid-1990s, more than three hundred African American churches were burned in the United States. Many of the burnings were done by white supremacist groups and Satanists. The Christian organization for men known as Promise Keepers has spent more than a million dollars in helping to rebuild and encourage black congregations around the country that were burned during that time period.

One church, in particular, had an interesting story. The pastor of the church was an African American man raised in the southern part of the country during turbulent racial times. He moved to a northern state to escape the pain of growing up in the segregated South. He worked hard, and slowly a vibrant congregation grew. One day, however, the work of arsonists completely destroyed the church building where his congregation met, and where he poured out his heart.

Knowing the arson was racially motivated, the pain and anger he left behind in the South found him once again in the North. Like many pastors of small African American churches, he not only was senior pastor, but also worked a full-time job to support his family and congregation. The church building needed to be renovated and he had mortgaged his home not long before the fire in order to fix and expand the church facility. In other words, all of his dreams and money went up in smoke . . . except for the pulpit! The pulpit was somehow preserved, kept perfectly intact.

Hurt, angry and bitter, he decided to quit the ministry. Nevertheless, one by one, his church family brought encouragement, and members of the Promise Keepers team came and gave about $20,000 toward the initial phase of getting back to preaching. After many days of doubting his call, and staring at that haunting pulpit, he decided to return to the ministry. He forgave the people who destroyed the church, rented a tent and got back behind the pulpit that had survived the flames. Before long, the incident received national attention, and people from around the country gave money to help rebuild. Promise Keepers was able to raise and give more than $100,000, and additional funds came from other donations.

While they met temporarily in the tent, plans were underway to rebuild. But, in the meantime an interesting thing happened. After hearing about the story on television, many whites came to hear the pastor speak—and many of them stayed. Before long, Hispanics and other races came in, too. As of 2006, this pastor is in a new debt-free building, with a racially and socially diverse congregation that has grown exponentially, both numerically and spiritually.

You see, his calling survived along with his pulpit, and God worked the bad with the good (see Romans 8:28) and propelled this congregation into His purpose at the threshing floor. Jeremiah 15:19 (NASB) says,

> Therefore thus says the LORD, "If you return, then I will restore you. Before Me you will stand; and if you extract the precious from the worthless, you will become My spokesman."

As you can see, we do not always go to the threshing floor or experience adverse times because of personal sin. But if we allow Him, God will use our adverse seasons to propel us to deeper places of intimacy with Him and further our callings. The pastor of this church, like Joseph, became God's spokesman who returned to the Lord and extracted the precious from the worthless. God took a seemingly worthless situation and left a precious pulpit because He knew His message of redemption, purpose, unity and love would be carried through this threshing-floor experience. God preserved the pulpit, to say, essentially, "The enemy may have destroyed your building, but you still have a voice." The result has been the salvation of souls, because this pastor was willing to worship the Lord in the midst of his hard place and be transformed. God used his bad situation as a platform for him to stand on, and left a pulpit for him to preach behind. And because of that, others have come to the Rock of salvation, just as in Joseph's day.

Joseph's personal transformation affected Egypt. Because of the transformation they saw in Joseph's life, many Egyptians came with him to the threshing floor—so many that they called the place Abelmizraim, which means "the mourning of the Egyptians":

> And they came to the threshingfloor of Atad, which is beyond Jordan, and there they mourned with a great and very sore lamentation: and he made a mourning for his father seven days. And when the inhabitants of the land, the Canaanites, saw the mourning in the floor of Atad, they said, This is a grievous mourning to the Egyptians: wherefore the name of it was called Abelmizraim, which is beyond Jordan.
>
> Genesis 50:10–11 KJV

According to Genesis 50:7, these were servants of Pharaoh and all the elders of the house of Egypt. They represent for us those who see the transformation in our lives and, in response, are drawn to and connect with the God we serve. Joseph's transformation on the threshing floor brought a harvest to the threshing floor, and a company of Egyptians came to the Rock of salvation.

I sense that God is doing the same with you. God is transforming you for the harvest that is about to come and making you a voice. The brokenness in your life is releasing His glory through you, and this transformation will bring glory to God and transform others. The threshing floor is where the precious is extracted from the worthless and you become God's spokesman, so you can be on your mountain of influence, but not of it.

> God is transforming you for the harvest that is about to come and making you a voice.

Threshed for Kingdom Influence

Like the wheat and chaff, God is throwing you into the wind. The winds of change in life seem to blow hard as God winnows our hearts. But while you are suspended in the air, and feeling vulnerable, use this time to ascend to new heights of abandoned worship to God. Let the winds blow away the chaff and everything that hinders the free flow of love from your heart to Him. Let God blow away everything not connected to the real you, the true essence of who you are in Christ.

If you are going through this, you probably feel more vulnerable than ever in your life, and are asking questions like: "God, where are You in all of this? What happened to my business? What happened to my marriage? What happened to my friendships? God, what happened to my ministry, and Your plans over my life? God, where are You?" You are like that kernel of wheat being thrown up into the air so that the chaff—all the props of life—can be blown away. Yes, relationships will be broken, and some of them will change. No, you may not have caused this, but God is using this situation to separate you to Himself in a very deep way.

You did not know it, but the deep longing of the Father's heart is responding to you. Most people are afraid of the pain of separating hurtful issues from their hearts. God, therefore, has brought about a circumcision not of human hands and is moving you to a new level of purity, holiness and intimacy (see Colossians 2:11). The weight of His glory inside you will safely land you back down on the Rock, who takes you from glory to glory as you worship Him in the midst of your hard place. You do not realize it now, but you are becoming a person of character, weight and substance, and like that weighty kernel of wheat, you will cut through the winds of adversity and will come back down to the Rock of salvation. He will sustain you.

He is also sealing His image upon you, and through your suffering, you are becoming more like Him. After you get through this, you will be sealed, no longer to be robbed in this area of your life. As a result, you are conformed into Christ's image, and your mind is molded by God instead of by the world system you are called to influence. Beloved, God is marking you. One day, your harvest will come, and when it does, you will come back to the memory of this hard place—your threshing floor—and worship, like Joseph, for the harvest that God provided you and others.

Jesus went through the same process. His threshing began in the Garden of Gethsemane in prayer, on the Mount of Olives, as he wept and sweated drops of blood (see Luke 22:44). His threshing was completed on the cross, on top of a mountain, as He laid down His life for us all. The beauty is that He rose for us also, and on that same mount, where He was threshed in prayer, something powerful is going to happen:

> In that day His feet will stand on the Mount of Olives, which is in front of Jerusalem on the east; and the Mount of Olives will be split in its middle from east to west.
>
> Zechariah 14:4 NASB

On the Mount of Olives, where He ascended into the sky, as described in Acts 1:9–12, so He is going to descend, like weighty wheat, and the fullness of His influence will be known to all. Before His ascension, Jesus walked the earth in humility, so as not to disturb His creation. But according to Zechariah 14:4, when He descends this time on the Mount of Olives, the mountain will split in half because of the sheer weight of Jesus' authority and influence. Listen: He will not be the size of a one-hundred-foot giant but will have the stature of a normal man. Yet, when He steps on the Mount of Olives, His weight, His authority and His influence will be fully known as His foot lands, and the entire mountain will split in half. Zechariah goes on to say,

> Then the LORD, my God, will come, and all the holy ones with Him! In that day there will be no light; the luminaries will dwindle. For it will be a unique day which is known to the LORD, neither day nor night, but it will come about that at evening time there will be light.
>
> Zechariah 14:5–7 NASB

Jesus Christ, the Light of the world, will become the source of light for the entire world. I love that it says "the luminaries will dwindle." In the natural, there will never be night again, and "luminaries," the moon and stars, will no longer be necessary. *Luminary* refers not only to heavenly bodies, but also to people known and exalted by the world as dignitaries. On this day, all, from the luminaries to the Illuminati, will have to bow the knee and declare out of either adoration or humiliation that Jesus

Christ is Lord, to the glory of God the Father (see Philippians 2:10–11). You see, there is no need for stars and celebrities to shine when the Son is out!

It also says "the holy ones will be with Him," and if you are a believing overcomer, that is you! Every tear will be wiped away from your eyes, and all your pain will make sense on that glorious day (see Revelation 21:4). And the knowledge of His glory, or weight of His influence, shall not end. Then, the most influential mountain of all will be established. Isaiah 2:2–4 says,

> And it shall come to pass in the last days, that the mountain of the LORD's house shall be established in the top of the mountains, and shall be exalted above the hills; and all nations shall flow unto it. And many people shall go and say, Come ye, and let us go up to the mountain of the LORD, to the house of the God of Jacob; and he will teach us of his ways, and we will walk in his paths: for out of Zion shall go forth the law, and the word of the LORD from Jerusalem. And he shall judge among the nations, and shall rebuke many people: and they shall beat their swords into plowshares, and their spears into pruninghooks: nation shall not lift up sword against nation, neither shall they learn war any more. O house of Jacob, come ye, and let us walk in the light of the LORD.
>
> Isaiah 2:2–5 KJV

Until then, beloved, occupy! (See Luke 19:13.) People who have been transformed by God can be used by Him to transform culture. Influence the mountain you are called to, and do not let it influence you. You were created for influence, to partner with God and change the world.

EXERCISING INFLUENCE *through Prayer*

Lord, You endured betrayal, hurt and pain at the deepest level. You were threshed on the cross for us all, and trusted Father God to make sense of Your question, "My God, My God, why hast Thou forsaken Me?" You laid it all down for us, and I choose to lay down my hurt, resentment and unresolved questions, my Friend and my Lord. I choose to trust that Your thoughts are higher than ours, and Your ways are higher as well.

Father, thank You for processing our pain, and making sense of our lives at the threshing floor. Though many are the afflictions of the righteous, truly You deliver us out of them all. All things do work together for our good, when we love You and are called according to Your purpose. And in spite of all I have gone through, I love You, and I choose to forgive and release those who have hurt me. I also forgive myself, for when I have let myself down. Whatever pain and adversity in my life, caused by me, or permitted by You, I grant You permission, God, to use it for Your glory.

What the enemy meant for evil, now use for Your good. I choose to extract the precious from the worthless, that I might become a change agent for You. As often as necessary, O God, thresh out of my heart and life everything that hinders intimacy between You and me. Under the influence of Your love, I ask that You make me an influence for Your Kingdom, in whatever capacity You see fit.

For Yours is the Kingdom, and Yours is the power, and Yours is the glory, for ever and ever. In Jesus name, Amen.

Index

call of to be a holy nation, 225, 226
Joseph's authority over, 245, 246
and the scandal of Absalom, 20, 22
and Sisera, 40–41

Jackson, Jesse, 180
Jacobs, Judy, 145
Jael, 40, 41
James, 50
  death of, 191
Jehu, 166–67, 180
Jeremiah, 224–25, 253
Jerry Maguire (1996), 57–58
Jesus Christ
  as the anointed one, 106, 120
  authority of, 28
  birth of, 171
  as bridegroom/Bridegroom King, 60,
    62, 118–19, 120
  conquering of His foes on the Cross,
    118
  death of, 63
  fragrance of, 104, 120
  friendship of with Martha and Mary,
    69–70
  humiliation of, 257–58
  humility of, 257
  Kingdom of, 120–21
  love of, 29, 71, 78, 128, 178, 189
  as the Morning Star, 51, 97, 98
  non-celebrity status of, 50
  and the "nothing in me" statement, 243
  obedience of, 76
  temptation of, 242
  and the weight of His glory, 126–30
Jesus Movement, 223
Jezebel, 161–64, 165, 166–67, 168, 172
Jezebelic influence, 159, 167, 169
Jim Crow laws, 95, 232
John (apostle), 69
John the Baptist, 179, 247–48
Jonathan, 67–68, 69, 72, 74
Joseph
  authority of over Israel, 245, 246
  dreams of, 245
  effect of on Egypt, 254–55
  and Potiphar's wife (handling of the
    enemy), 246–48

Joshua, 44
joy, 76, 118, 119, 143
  Kingdom joy, 154
justice, 231–32
Justice House of Prayer (Washington,
  D.C.), 192–93, 198

kabod (Hebrew: "weighty presence"),
  126
Keath, Greg, 168
Kennedy, John F., 151
kettle, 73–74
King, Martin Luther, Jr., 98, 138–39,
  157, 158, 180, 218
kingdom of darkness (Satan), 28, 37, 51,
  59, 84, 89, 105, 126, 140, 150, 161,
  215
  clash of with the Kingdom of light,
    20–23
  influence of, 45–46, 48, 49, 172, 197
  and music, 145–46
  and "thrones of iniquity," 197
Kingdom of light (God), 24, 32, 37, 43,
  47, 126
  clash of with the kingdom of
    darkness, 20–23
  influence of, 150, 189
kings, 116, 117, 121, 195, 244
Kinsey, Alfred, 215

labab (Hebrew: "stolen my heart"),
  62, 67
Las Vegas, 188, 189
laughter, 160
laws, of influence, 21, 22
Lazarus, 70
leadership, 44, 196, 239
  mountaintop leaders, 241–42
Leary, Timothy, 215
leaven, 48, 49, 139–42, 143, 150, 191, 204
Lee, Sharon, 133
legalism, 49, 141
lepers, 219–22
Levites, 127, 187, 189–90
Levitt, Steven, 170
Liddell, Eric, 226–27
logic, influence of, 82

William L. Ford III (better known as Will) is a nationally known businessman, author and minister. A graduate of Morehouse College in Atlanta and Emmaus Road Ministry School in Euless, Texas, he is founder of Will Ford Ministries. Will travels extensively throughout the U.S., speaking in churches and conferences on prayer, unity, revival and marketplace transformation. He currently serves as director of the Marketplace Leadership major at Christ For The Nations Institute in Dallas, Texas.

He has been interviewed by CBS News, has been featured on *The 700 Club* and has appeared in Christian magazines. He is the co-author, along with Dutch Sheets, of *History Makers: Your Prayers Have Power to Heal the Past and Shape the Future*. Will's passion is to see the expanding influence of Christ's love in every nation through united prayer and involvement for societal transformation.

Will and his wife, Dehavilland, are the proud parents of Joshua, Amanda and Benjamin. The Fords reside in Dallas, Texas.

You may contact Will Ford at:

Christ For The Nations Institute
214-302-6497
email: marketplacedirector@cfni.org or
wwillford@gmail.com